THIRTY-ONE

DAYS

OF

PEACE

Living the Life of God's Peace

SCOTT REECE

© 2021 by Scott Reece

Published by Kindle Direct a division of Amazon Publishing Seattle, Washington, www.kdp.amazon.com

ISBN-13: 978-1976095092

Library of Congress Cataloging-in-Publication Data is on file at the Library of Congress, Washington, DC.

Unless otherwise noted, all scriptures are taken from the New King James Version®. Copyright © 1982 by Thomas Nelson, Inc. Used by permission. All rights reserved.

DEDICATION

In the summer of 2015, my family was forever changed. God
sovereignly joined us together with a church body that lovingly
embraced us as one of their own. From the very first day, it was as if
we were "born and raised here." The love, kindness and generosity
of MGT (Moline Gospel Temple) New Hope Church has been
overwhelming to say the least. Your passion and purpose for Jesus
and this community through the years is nothing less than short of
amazing. We consider it a great privilege to journey with you in life
as we serve Jesus and one another.

Thank you for loving us and thank you for making it easy to serve.
You have found a place in our hearts that is eternal. This book is
dedicated to you, and may it be used of God to bring peace to your
hearts and lives, all the days of your life.
Remember, we walk by faith and not by sight.

Table of Contents

Thirty-One Days of Peace

Introduction

Perfect Peace is always the will of God. One of the names of God that defines the essence of who He is, as well as His character is Jehovah-Shalom. Nothing is missing, nothing is lacking. Your peace is a primary target of the enemy. If he can remove you from peace, you will become susceptible to his attacks. Your peace is a stronghold, a formidable weapon against the strategic lies of Satan. The world does not know this kind of peace and neither does it understand it. We are constantly being barraged with elements of a false peace and security that ultimately end up leaving you empty and void. Your peace is so important to God that it is actually a vital part of the redemptive price that Jesus paid on your behalf. "The chastisement of your peace was laid upon Him" (Isaiah 53:5). Your peace has been bought and paid for, so why not walk in it? Plant yourself firmly in the Word of peace, surrender to the Prince of peace and walk in the Power of peace…it is yours today.

100 Scriptures on Peace

1. I have spoken these things that you might have peace.
(John 16:33).

2. To be spiritually minded is life and peace.
(Romans 8:6).

3. And let the peace of God rule in your hearts, to which also you were called in one body; and be thankful. (Colossians 3:15).

4. God is our refuge and strength, a very present help in trouble.
(Psalm 46:1).

5. It is God who arms me with strength and makes my way perfect. He makes my feet like the feet of deer and sets me on my high places. He teaches my hands to make war, so that my arms can bend a bow of bronze. You have also given me the shield of your salvation; your right hand has held me up, your gentleness has made me great. You enlarged my path under me, so my feet did not slip. (Psalm 18:32-36).

6. Great peace have those who love your law, And nothing causes them to stumble. (Psalm 119:165).

7. Fear not, for I am with you; be not dismayed, for I am your God. I will strengthen you, yes, I will help you, and I will uphold you with my righteous right hand. (Isaiah 41:10).

8. Be strong and of good courage, do not fear nor be afraid of them; for the LORD your God, He is the One who goes with you. He will not leave you nor forsake you. (Deuteronomy 31:6).

9. Peace I leave with you, My peace I give to you; not as the world gives do I give to you. Let not your heart be troubled, neither let it be afraid. (John 14:27).

10. But the fruit of the Spirit is love, joy, peace, longsuffering, kindness, goodness, faithfulness, gentleness, and self-control. Against such there is no law. And those who are Christ's have crucified the flesh with its passions and desires. If we live in the Spirit, let us also walk in the Spirit. Let us not become conceited, provoking one another, envying one another. (Galatians 5:22-26).

11. Now may our Lord Jesus Christ Himself, and our God and Father, who has loved us and given us everlasting consolation and good hope by grace, comfort your hearts and establish you in every good word and work. (2 Thessalonians 2:16-17).

12. Speak to Aaron and his sons, saying, this is the way you shall bless the children of Israel. Say to them: the LORD bless you and keep you; the LORD make His face shine upon you and be gracious

to you; the LORD lift up His countenance upon you and give you peace. (Numbers 6:23-26).

13. O LORD, You are the portion of my inheritance and my cup; you maintain my lot. The lines have fallen to me in pleasant places; yes, I have a good inheritance. I will bless the LORD who has given me counsel; my heart also instructs me in the night seasons. I have set the LORD always before me; because He is at my right hand I shall not be moved. (Psalm 16:5-8).

14. The LORD will give strength to His people; the LORD will bless His people with peace. (Psalm 29:11).

15. The LORD is my light and my salvation; whom shall I fear? The LORD is the strength of my life; of whom shall I be afraid? (Psalm 27:1).

16. For God has not given us a spirit of fear, but of power and of love and of a sound mind. (2 Timothy 1:7).

17. Be anxious for nothing, but in everything by prayer and supplication, with thanksgiving, let your requests be made known to God; and the peace of God, which surpasses all understanding, will guard your hearts and minds through Christ Jesus. (Philippians 4:6-7).

18. Therefore, having been justified by faith, we have peace with God through our Lord Jesus Christ, through whom also we have

access by faith into this grace in which we stand, and rejoice in hope of the glory of God. (Romans 5:1-2).

19. Now may the God of hope fill you with all joy and peace in believing, that you may abound in hope by the power of the Holy Spirit. (Romans 15:13).

20. But He was wounded for our transgressions, He was bruised for our iniquities; the chastisement for our peace was upon Him, and by His stripes we are healed. (Isaiah 53:5).

21. Let not your heart be troubled; you believe in God, believe also in Me. In My Father's house are many mansions; if it were not so, I would have told you. I go to prepare a place for you. And if I go and prepare a place for you, I will come again and receive you to myself; that where I am, there you may be also. (John 14:1-3).

22. Cast your burden on the LORD, and He shall sustain you; He shall never permit the righteous to be moved. (Psalm 55:22).

23. Therefore we do not lose heart. Even though our outward man is perishing, yet the inward man is being renewed day by day. For our light affliction, which is but for a moment, is working for us a far more exceeding and eternal weight of glory, while we do not look at the things which are seen, but at the things which are not seen. For the things, which are, seen are temporary, but the things, which are not seen, are eternal. (2 Corinthians 4:16-18).

24. He has made everything beautiful in its time. Also He has put eternity in their hearts, except that no one can find out the work that God does from beginning to end. (Ecclesiastes 3:11).

25. Now may the Lord of peace Himself give you peace always in every way. The Lord be with you all. (2 Thessalonians 3:16).

26. For unto us a Child is born, unto us a Son is given; and the government will be upon His shoulder. And His name will be called Wonderful, Counselor, Mighty God, Everlasting Father, Prince of Peace. (Isaiah 9:6).

27. For the mountains shall depart, and the hills be removed, but My kindness shall not depart from you, nor shall My covenant of peace be removed," says the LORD, who has mercy on you. (Isaiah 54:10).

28. Come to Me, all you who labor and are heavy laden, and I will give you rest. Take My yoke upon you and learn from Me, for I am gentle and lowly in heart, and you will find rest for your souls. For my yoke is easy and my burden is light. (Matthew 11:28-30).

29. For the kingdom of God is not eating and drinking, but righteousness and peace and joy in the Holy Spirit. For he who serves Christ in these things is acceptable to God and approved by men. Therefore let us pursue the things, which make for peace and the things by which one may edify another. (Romans 14:17-19).

30. For your obedience has become known to all. Therefore I am glad on your behalf; but I want you to be wise in what is good, and simple concerning evil. And the God of peace will crush Satan under your feet shortly. The grace of our Lord Jesus Christ be with you. Amen. (Romans 16:19-20).

31. For we do not wrestle against flesh and blood, but against principalities, against powers, against the rulers of the darkness of this age, against spiritual hosts of wickedness in the heavenly places. Therefore take up the whole armor of God, that you may be able to withstand in the evil day, and having done all, to stand. Stand therefore, having girded your waist with truth, having put on the breastplate of righteousness, and having shod your feet with the preparation of the gospel of peace; above all, taking the shield of faith with which you will be able to quench all the fiery darts of the wicked one. And take the helmet of salvation, and the sword of the Spirit, which is the word of God. (Ephesians 6:12-17).

32. Pursue peace with all people, and holiness, without which no one will see the Lord. (Hebrews 12:14).

33. Let him turn away from evil and do good; let him seek peace and pursue it. (1 Peter 3:11).

34. Casting all your care upon Him, for He cares for you. (1 Peter 5:7).

35. See that no one renders evil for evil to anyone, but always pursue what is good both for yourselves and for all. (1 Thessalonians 5:15).

36. Now the fruit of righteousness is sown in peace by those who make peace. (James 3:18).

37. Deceit is in the heart of those who devise evil, but counselors of peace have joy. (Proverbs 12:20).

38. When a man's ways please the LORD, he makes even his enemies to be at peace with him. (Proverbs 16:7).

39. If it is possible, as much as depends on you, live peaceably with all men. (Romans 12:18).

40. Depart from evil and do good; seek peace and pursue it. (Psalm 34:14).

41. Mercy, peace and love be yours in abundance. (Jude 1:2).

42. Not returning evil for evil or reviling for reviling, but on the contrary blessing, knowing that you were called to this, that you may inherit a blessing. For "He who would love life and see good days, Let him refrain his tongue from evil, and his lips from speaking deceit. Let him turn away from evil and do good; let him seek peace and pursue it. (1 Peter 3:9-11).

43. Mark the blameless man and observe the upright; for the future of that man is peace. (Psalm 37:37).

44. I will hear what God the LORD will speak, For He will speak peace to His people and to His saints; but let them not turn back to folly. (Psalm 85:8).

45. Repay no one evil for evil. Have regard for good things in the sight of all men. If it is possible, as much as depends on you, live peaceably with all men. Beloved, do not avenge yourselves, but rather give place to wrath; for it is written, "Vengeance is Mine, I will repay," says the Lord. Therefore "If your enemy is hungry, feed him; If he is thirsty, give him a drink; for in so doing you will heap coals of fire on his head." Do not be overcome by evil but overcome evil with good. (Romans 12:17-21).

46. You will keep him in perfect peace, whose mind is stayed on You, because he trusts in You. (Isaiah 2:3).

47. LORD, You will establish peace for us, For You have also done all our works in us. (Isaiah 26:12).

48. For you shall go out with joy and be led out with peace; the mountains and the hills shall break forth into singing before you, and all the trees of the field shall clap their hands. (Isaiah 55:12).

49. May God himself, the God of peace, sanctify you through and through. May your whole spirit, soul and body be kept blameless at the coming of our Lord Jesus Christ. (1 Thessalonians 5:23).

50. For God is not the author of confusion but of peace, as in all the churches of the saints. (1 Corinthians 14:33).

51. Thus says the LORD of hosts: The fast of the fourth month, The fast of the fifth, The fast of the seventh, and the fast of the tenth, shall be joy and gladness and cheerful feasts for the house of Judah. Therefore love truth and peace. (Zechariah 8:19).

52. Flee also youthful lusts; but pursue righteousness, faith, love, and peace with those who call on the Lord out of a pure heart. (2 Timothy 2:22).

53. I am for peace. (Psalm 120:7).

54. Finally, brethren, farewell. Become complete. Be of good comfort, be of one mind, live in peace; and the God of love and peace will be with you. (2 Corinthians 13:11).

55. For Mordecai the Jew was second to King Ahasuerus and was great among the Jews and well received by the multitude of his brethren, seeking the good of his people and speaking peace to all his countrymen. (Esther 10:3).

56. Salt is good, but if the salt loses its flavor, how will you season it? Have salt in yourselves and have peace with one another. (Mark 9:50).

57. And to esteem them very highly in love for their work's sake. Be at peace among yourselves. (1 Thessalonians 5:13).

58. But the meek shall inherit the earth and shall delight themselves in the abundance of peace. (Psalm 37:11).

59. Mercy and truth have met together; Righteousness and peace have kissed. (Psalm 85:10).

60. Pray for the peace of Jerusalem: May they prosper who love you. (Psalm 122:6).

61. He makes peace in your borders, and fills you with the finest wheat. (Psalm 147:14).

62. My son, do not forget my law, but let your heart keep my commands; For length of days and long life and peace they will add to you. (Proverbs 3:1-2).

63. For I know the thoughts that I think toward you, says the LORD, thoughts of peace and not of evil, to give you a future and a hope. (Jeremiah 29:11).

64. Blessed are the peacemakers, for they shall be called sons of God. (Matthew 5:9).

65. Then, the same day at evening, being the first day of the week, when the doors were shut where the disciples were assembled, for

fear of the Jews, Jesus came and stood in the midst, and said to them, Peace be with you. (John 20:19).

66. To the elect according to the foreknowledge of God the Father, in sanctification of the Spirit, for obedience and sprinkling of the blood of Jesus Christ: Grace to you and peace be multiplied. (1 Peter 1:2).

67. Therefore, having been justified by faith, we have peace with God through our Lord Jesus Christ. (Romans 5:1).

68. But I say to you who hear: Love your enemies, do good to those who hate you. (Luke 6:27).

69. But if the unbeliever departs, let him depart; a brother or a sister is not under bondage in such cases. But God has called us to peace. (1 Corinthians 7:15).

70. Therefore I say to you, do not worry about your life, what you will eat or what you will drink; nor about your body, what you will put on. Is not life more than food and the body more than clothing? Look at the birds of the air, for they neither sow nor reap nor gather into barns; yet your heavenly Father feeds them. Are you not of more value than they? Which of you by worrying can add one cubit to his stature? (Matthew 6:25-27).

71. Therefore do not worry about tomorrow, for tomorrow will worry about it is own things. Sufficient for the day is it is own trouble. (Matthew 6:34).

72. And which of you by worrying can add one cubit to his stature? (Luke 12:25).

73. Yea, though I walk through the valley of the shadow of death, I will fear no evil; for you are with your rod; your staff, and me they comfort me. (Psalm 23:4).

74. But now, thus says the LORD, who created you, O Jacob, and He who formed you, O Israel: "Fear not, for I have redeemed you; I have called you by your name; You are Mine. When you pass through the waters, I will be with you; and through the rivers, they shall not overflow you. When you walk through the fire, you shall not be burned, nor shall the flame scorch you. For I am the LORD your God, the Holy One of Israel, your Savior. (Isaiah 43:1-3).

75. So we may boldly say: "The LORD is my helper; I will not fear. What can man do to me?"
(Hebrews 13:6).

76. Whenever I am afraid, I will trust in you. (Psalm 56:3).

77. I will lift up my eyes to the hills— from whence comes my help? My help comes from the LORD, who made heaven and earth. (Psalm 121:1-2).

78. Trust in the LORD with all your heart and lean not on your own understanding; In all your ways acknowledge Him, and He shall direct your paths. (Proverbs 3:5-6).

79. What then shall we say to these things? If God is for us, who can be against us? (Romans 8:31).

80. Through whom also we have access by faith into this grace in which we stand and rejoice in hope of the glory of God. And not only that, but we also glory in tribulations, knowing that tribulation produces perseverance; and perseverance, character; and character, hope. Now hope does not disappoint, because the love of God has been poured out in our hearts by the Holy Spirit who was given to us. (Romans 5:2-5).

81. For we were saved in this hope, but hope that is seen is not hope; for why does one still hope for what he sees? But if we hope for what we do not see, we eagerly wait for it with perseverance. (Romans 8:24-25).

82. Rejoicing in hope, patient in tribulation, continuing steadfastly in prayer. (Romans 12:12).

83. For whatever things were written before were written for our learning, that we through the patience and comfort of the Scriptures might have hope. (Romans 15:4).

84. The LORD your God in your midst, the Mighty One, will save; He will rejoice over you with gladness, He will quiet you with His love, He will rejoice over you with singing." (Zephaniah 3:17).

85. Jesus answered and said to her, "Whoever drinks of this water will thirst again, but whoever drinks of the water that I shall give him will never thirst. But the water that I shall give him will become in him a fountain of water springing up into everlasting life." (John 14:3-4).

86. Seek the LORD and His strength; seek His face evermore. (1 Chronicles 16:11).

87. And since we have the same spirit of faith, according to what is written, "I believed and therefore I spoke," we also believe and therefore speak, knowing that He who raised up the Lord Jesus will also raise us up with Jesus, and will present us with you. (2 Corinthians 4:13-14).

88. Be still and know that I am God; I will be exalted among the nations; I will be exalted in the earth. (Psalm 46:10).

89. And He said to her, "Daughter, your faith has made you well. Go in peace and be healed of your affliction." (Mark 5:34).

90. "Glory to God in the highest, and on earth peace, goodwill toward men." (Luke 2:14).

91. Then He said to the woman, "Your faith has saved you. Go in peace." (II Timothy 4:18).

92. Blessed is the King who comes in the name of the LORD. Peace in heaven and glory in the highest. (Luke 19:38).

93. Now as they said these things, Jesus Himself stood in the midst of them, and said to them, "Peace to you." (Luke 24:36).

94. So Jesus said to them again, "Peace to you. As the Father has sent Me, I also send you." (John 20:21).

95. The word which God sent to the children of Israel, preaching peace through Jesus Christ, He is Lord of all. (Acts 10:36).

96. But glory, honor, and peace to everyone who works what is good, to the Jew first and also to the Greek. (Romans 2:10).

97. Now the God of peace be with you all. Amen. (Romans 15:33).

98. For God is not the author of confusion but of peace, as in all the churches of the saints. (1 Corinthians 14:33).

99. For God is not the author of confusion but of peace, as in all the churches of the saints. (2 Corinthians 13:11).

100. Grace to you and peace from God the Father and our Lord Jesus Christ. (Galatians 1:3).

Day One
PEACE THAT OVERCOMES

"I have told you these things so that in me you may have peace. In this world, you will have trouble. But take heart. I have overcome the world."

John 16:33

The disciples of Jesus find themselves on the brink of some pretty radical changes in their world. Their lives have already been turned upside down by the life and ministry of Jesus, and now He startles them with a conversation of His pending departure. They never expected it all to end this early, and neither did they anticipate the level of responsibility they would be carrying. Soon, they will be facing a lot of pressure and carrying a weight that they were not ready for. Ever been there?

We have all been put in situations like that. We have all received a report that was completely unexpected and not necessarily good news. Often, our immediate reaction is based on our emotions, and we respond in anger, confusion, fear, and even pride. Knowing that His disciples would have to deal with all of those issues, He prepared them by "speaking the Word" to them. He was preparing them spiritually for what they would face in the natural. Jesus not only foretold what they would encounter, but He reminded them that real peace was the result of an intimate relationship with Him. Peace does not come from being emotionally stable or from having your world perfectly organized. It is the result of a deep, abiding relationship with Christ.

Lessons of Peace

The Centrality of Christ: When you are grounded in life with Christ, the world around you cannot disturb what is going on inside of you. Jesus said, "*In Me, you might have peace.*" I have often heard people say that Christ wants to be first in your life, but in actuality, He wants to be "central" in your life. Whenever He is simply "first," everything that follows is decidedly disconnected. If you make Him central in your life, then everything is connected to your life in Christ. The centrality of Christ is the source of your peace, and that is what it means to make Jesus the Lord of your life.

The Tranquility of Peace: So, what is peace, exactly? Many adjectives describe the characteristics of peace, but is it an emotion, a state of mind, a condition of the heart? It is all of the above, but most importantly, it results from a personal relationship with Jesus Christ. In today's reading, the Greek word for peace is "Eirene," which means "tranquility, to be exempt from the havoc of war, harmony, security, safety, and prosperity." You must take note of the fact that Jesus was preparing His disciples for the difficulties that they would face in the natural, and that the literal definition of peace is "exemption from the havoc of war", not war itself. In other words, you cannot control the issues that might swirl around you, but when you are walking in peace, those circumstances cannot remove you from your place of peace.

Be of Good Cheer: We live in a fallen world and every single day you and I are forced to deal with the effects and residue of that fall. Jesus told His disciples that we would have tribulation. It means to be "pressed, to experience pressure, sometimes oppression, affliction, and distress." After all of that, He tells His disciples to "be of good cheer." Seriously? It means to have courage and confidence.

So, in the face of life pressures, oppression that might arise, afflictions, and even distress, be courageous and be confident. How can Jesus make such a statement? The very next thing that He say is: "I have overcome the world." All the power of your foe has been defeated, temptation no longer has control over you, and even death has been defeated on your behalf. You are victorious in life because Jesus was victorious.

Now you know why He tells us to be at peace. Our victory lies in His strength, in the fact that he defeated death, hell, and the grave, and that we are no longer subject to the lies, strategies, and defeat of the enemy. Oppression, distress, and affliction do not have to overwhelm us. As we find ourselves rooted and grounded in our relationship with Jesus, we can rise in faith and lay hold of the peace that He alone promises.

Today's Confession of Peace

My peace is not of this world. As I am rooted and grounded in Christ and have experienced the redeeming power of His love at work in my life, I stand today on the promise of peace.

Even though I may be surrounded with oppression, tribulations, trials, and afflictions, I will not be moved. What is going on in the world around me does not have the power or the ability to disrupt the peace that I have in Christ.

My mind is at peace, and I will not be tormented. My heart is at peace, and I am secure and safe, my emotions are at peace, and I am tranquil and exempt from the "havoc of war" surrounding me on every side.

Jesus is Lord over my mind, my will, and my emotions, and I walk in divine peace and harmony.

Day Two

THE PEACE OF SURRENDER

"So letting your sinful nature control your mind leads to death. But letting the Spirit control your mind leads to life and peace."

Romans 8:6

We live in a world that consists of two kingdoms. The first is the Kingdom of God, which according to Romans 8:2, is governed by "the law of life that is in Christ Jesus." The second kingdom is one of darkness which is governed by the law of sin and death. The kingdom of darkness specializes in masking the hidden issues that lurk just beneath the surface. Appealing to the sinful nature, the natural man's desires and longings are constantly luring and drawing to a life that ultimately leads to bondage, deception, and even death. The appeal of the sinful nature is sensuality and a promise that there are no consequences for actions. However, nothing could be further from the truth. There is no middle ground; sin wants ultimate control and is always seeking the upper hand. The only problem is that sin comes with a very high price, the nature of death, and ultimately, death itself.

Lessons Of Peace

You are A Spirit Being: Have you ever been around someone who is dying with no hope in promise of life and resurrection in Jesus? It is depressing and oppressive. There is no hope, no life, and no sense of promise or purpose. Whenever we allow sinful nature to rise and take control of our lives, the result is always an open the door to the spirit and nature of oppression, which is devoid of promise or purpose. The very nature of that lifestyle is the opposite of the peace that comes from living according to the law of life in Christ Jesus.

The very heart and center of man are his mind, his will, and his emotions. You are a spirit; you possess a soul, and you live in a body. Your spirit is the part of you that will live forever, and your soul is the part of you that primarily dictates your passions, desires, and appetites in life. That is the part of you that is constantly in a battle between light and darkness, right and wrong, what is moral and what is immoral. Whenever you allow your sinful desires to dictate your mind, will, and emotions, the result is always darkness and death.

The Zoe-Life of God: When you allow the Spirit to establish your thoughts, feelings, purposes, and intentions, the result is life and peace. The word "life" in Greek, is "Zoe," which means the absolute fullness of life, the blessing of life, a vigorous and active life that is only found in a relationship with Jesus Christ. So, the choice is yours; you can either allow your carnal and sinful nature to dictate how you think, feel and live, or let the Spirit be in control of your mind, leading to life and peace. It comes down to a life of surrender and resistance. Learning how to say no to the flesh and yes to the Spirit.

Today's Confession of Peace

My life consists of more than just the demands of my flesh or the cravings of the world around me. I have been bought with a great price, and Jesus gave His life so that I could live in peace and be free from the bondage of the carnal nature.

Today I confess that I am a child of God, and I have the mind of Christ. I hold fast to the thoughts, feelings, purposes, and intentions of Christ in all that I do, who I am, and even how I think.

I have the power and the ability to say no to sin and the cravings of carnality. I am strong in faith. I am what God says I am, and I live in peace, harmony, and by the life of Christ that is in me.

The absolute fullness of life is mine in Christ Jesus, and that which appeals to the lower nature of death and bondage does hold sway over me.

Day Three

THE UMPIRE

"And let the peace that comes from Christ rule in your hearts. For as members of one body, you are called to live in peace. And always be thankful."

Colossians 3:15

How do you make decisions? Most people get caught in the trap of weighing the pros and cons, stacking up the odds, and considering that which is most logical. In actuality, that is the door opened up for us by our ancestors in the Garden of Eden. Making decisions on that order is "eating from the tree of the knowledge of good and evil." Genesis 3:2-7, *"And the woman said to the serpent, "We may eat the fruit of the trees of the garden; but of the fruit of the tree which is in the midst of the garden, God has said, 'You shall not eat it, nor shall you touch it, lest you die.' Then the serpent said to the woman, "You will not surely die. For God knows that in the day you eat of it, your eyes will be opened, and you will be like God, knowing good and evil." So when the woman saw that the tree was good for food, that it was pleasant to the eyes, and a tree desirable to make one wise, she took of its fruit and ate. She also gave her husband with her, and he ate. Then the eyes of both of them were opened."*

Indeed, their eyes were opened, but it was according to carnal knowledge and reasoning.

Lessons Of Peace

The Power of Obedience: Before eating from the tree of knowledge, their decisions were made based on their relationship and obedience to God their Father. Before this act of disobedience, they were clothed by the glory of God, but His glory lifted, and their eyes were opened to the world of evil around them, and they saw themselves as naked. The fallout from this one action was astronomical and devastating. Today, many people make decisions based on the knowledge of good and evil and that which is logical to the natural man. So, what is wrong with that? The problem is that according to 2 Corinthians 11:14, Satan masquerades as an angel of light and can manipulate the elements of the flesh and the natural world. He can cause that which is right, seem wrong and that which is wrong seem right.

A Decision you can Trust: So, how do you make decisions that you can trust? I am glad you asked. That is what today's scripture reading is about. Paul tells us to "let the peace that comes from Christ rule in your hearts." There is security, harmony, safety, and even prosperity that is yours as a result of your relationship with Jesus Christ. It cannot be counterfeited, disguised, or replicated. No matter how difficult the decision, Christ wants you to make your decision from a place of peace (that comes from Him) and not from

31

logic or natural knowledge. The peace of God is the only way that you can be confident you are not being led astray.

Let His Peace Rule: To fully comprehend the power of this scripture, we need to unpack the word "rule." The Greek word is "brabeuo," and it means to decide, determine, direct, control, and rule. But that is not all; "brabeuo" literally means to allow the peace of God to serve as an umpire. In a baseball game, the umpire is the one who is carefully watching over the play and even in the most intense situation, makes a final call that is difficult to overturn. The player is called out or safe at the plate, and there is no point in arguing. That is the peace of God. No matter what it looks like in the natural, no matter what it feels like emotionally, no matter what others around you might say, if you violate the peace of God in your heart, you are making the wrong decision. "It just does not make sense," that is okay because we are not led by our mind, will, or emotions, but ultimately by the peace of God that comes from an abiding relationship with Christ.

Today's Confession of Peace

I am not moved by what I see, think, hear or feel. I am moved by what God says about me and by His abiding peace.

I make decisions by my relationship with Jesus Christ, and I refuse to make decisions based on what "seems" right or wrong or what is most logical.

My decisions are made based on the peace of God that rules in my heart and life, no matter how it may appear in the natural.

As I choose to abide in Christ, He takes in me to lead and guide me with His perfect peace. He promises to keep me in perfect peace when my mind is stayed on Him.

Day Four

AN EVER-PRESENT HELP

"God is our refuge and strength, an ever-present help in trouble."

Psalms 46:1

"When peace like a river, attendeth my way, When sorrows like sea billows roll." ("When Peace Like a River," Philip Paul Bliss). Have you ever been in trouble and felt like nobody was there for you? I think we have all been in that place where we felt isolated and left on our own to fend for ourselves. The truth is that as a believer, you are never alone, and God is always ready, willing, and able to rescue you and to be an "ever-present" help in the time of need. This is not only an encouraging verse but also a strong declaration of who God is in your life. He declares Himself to be your shelter from the storms of life that gather against you. He is also your protector from danger, as well as falsehood. This scripture is an invitation from God to put your trust, confidence, and hope (expectancy) in Him. He promises that if you will put your trust in Him, He will cause you to prevail and will strengthen you regardless of the situation.

Lessons Of Peace

A Very-Present Help: The Lord uses the strength of words to describe precisely who He is so that whenever you are faced with troubles or difficulties, you can have a point of reference that will always lead you back to a place of divine peace. God is not only your refuge and strength; He is also a "very-present" help in times of trouble. The phrase "very-present" makes it very clear that He's "got your back." The Hebrew word is "meod," which means to be exceeding, in abundance, and a strong force. The peace of God is much more than a calming emotion when life rages against you. God is peace, His presence is peace, His Spirit is peace, and He is a strong force against anything contrary to His purposes, aligned against you. This is the peace that brings comfort in your life as well as a sense of security. Because your God is unshakeable and unmovable, so are you. I can declare with confidence that regardless of the circumstances that have been aligned against me, I will not be afraid, I will not be moved, and I will not be taken out of my peace. Even when I am faced with distress, or my adversary unleashes a barrage of oppression against me, it is in the peace of God that I discover my refuge, and it is in that peace that I find a strength that is found nowhere else.

Today's Confession of Peace

Your peace is my refuge and my strength. Your peace is my hope. When the rivers rage against me, I will not be moved, and I will not rise in fear. Today, I hide in the shelter of your peace, and I stand in a place of security knowing that you "have my back." I thank you, Father, that you will go above and beyond and that your peace will flow upon my life in abundance and strength.

Day Five

HIND'S FEET IN HIGH PLACES

"It is God who arms me with strength and makes my way perfect. He makes my feet like the feet of a deer; he enables me to stand on the heights. He trains my hands for battle; my arms can bend a bow of bronze. You give me your shield of victory, and your right hand sustains me; you stoop down to make me great. You broaden the path beneath me so that my ankles do not turn."

Psalm 18:32-36

The peace of God in your life is much more than an emotion. God will literally "gird" you with His peace and give you a supernatural strength that can come from nowhere else. God's peace results from healthy spirituality and soundness of soul, which is an undisturbed composure amid a chaotic and confusing world. When you walk in the supernatural peace of God, He "makes your way perfect," or in other words, He brings a "completeness" to your life that transcends the disturbing ways around you. God is calling you to the high places in life; those places that lift you above the distractions and the ungodly noise of a life and a world that is easily dictated by the sound of many waters.

Lessons of Peace

A Battle-Strategy of Peace: When peace becomes a part of your battle strategy, you set yourself up for victory even against the greatest of foes because the enemy has no counterfeit or effective weapon against the peace of God. It is by His peace that God confirms and establishes you. It's where you find a supernatural assurance of His continual presence, no matter what life may look like or what might confront you at any given time. The peace of God is both safe and strong. In His peace, you are removed from the reach of the enemy and situated in a secure place, surrounded by the armies of God. God's peace is not just a protective emotion when the turmoil of life rages; it is a weapon that God will use to protect you and to bring you victory on the day of battle.

His peace is a stronghold in which the believer finds protection and defense against the world's clamor and the anxiety that comes with it. The peace of God is also an offensive weapon that can be easily used to establish and command the stronghold of God and give a much more significant advantage in possessing territory that the enemy has previously held.

Standing in High Places: Anxiety will cause insecurity and promote a lack of steadfastness, whereas the peace of God will cause you to stand in faith and confidence and not be moved by what you see, think, hear or feel. The peace of God will look beyond what you can see in the natural and will discern the root of turmoil.

Peace is not moved by anxiety, turmoil, fear, or the lies of the enemy. You will stand in high places with confident security that can only come from the peace of God.

Today's Confession of Peace

Today, I will allow the peace of God to overflow my mind, my will, and my emotions. I will not be moved by what I see, think, hear or feel.

Like the deer stands in the high places and is not afraid of falling or stumbling, I stand in the peace of God and find strength for the battle that is before me.

Even though confusion, chaos, and anxiety encompass me on every side, I am not moved, and my composure is not disturbed. I stand in the stronghold of peace, and I rise to possess the territory that is rightfully mine.

Day Six

THE PEACE OF THE WORD

"Great peace have those who love your law, and nothing can make
them stumble."
Psalm 119:165

When you read the Bible, you are not just reading literature penned by great men of God; you are reading God, Himself. From the pages of your Bible flow the divine character and attributes of God. The purposes and the passions of God are revealed in His Word and become life to those that love it. The "secret" behind captivating the life of the Word is not just reading it but loving it. Loving God's Word is coming to a place of thirst and hunger for His Word and finding a dependency on His Word that nothing else can satisfy. How can a person be in love with a book? That is the answer; the Bible is not just a book. It is revelation; it is love made manifest, a life of success and destiny, penned by the hand of men who received divine inspiration.

Lessons of Peace

God is in Control: There are many benefits found in loving the Word, among which is the peace of God. Peace flows from the Word when it is received in faith. As the Word of God washes over your mind, will and emotions, it brings a sense of divine and perfect security and wholeness. The Word's central message is that God is ultimately in control; all things are under His hand and authority, and He will never leave you or forsake you. He promises that He is with you always and that He has already made a way for you, regardless of what you might be facing. When you begin to receive that, believe that, walk in it, and declare it, the result is the ever-present peace of God that flows out of your spirit, into your mind, will, and emotions and manifests itself in all that pertains to you. The peace of God is the mountain, the turmoil of life is the wind, and no matter how hard the wind might blow or howl, the mountain will not be moved.

The Peace that Supernaturally Exceeds: Please notice that we are not just talking about peace; we are talking about "great" peace. The Hebrew word for great is "Rab," meaning abounding, more numerous than, abundant, more than enough, strong, greater than, and exceeding. I think I get the picture: no matter what I am going through, the peace of God supernaturally surpasses, excels, and transcends my circumstances. You cannot wait until you are in the midst of the battle to run to the Word and try to find peace. The best time to walk and establish peace in your life is when you are not faced with life's struggles. In other words, get ready in advance, and when the battle arises, you will be prepared.

Today's Confession of Peace

I love the Word of God. I am a student of the Word, I am a person of the Word, and the Word of God dictates how I think, how I live, and who I am.

The strength of the Word surrounds me, and the peace of God that comes from my understanding of who I am flows out of every aspect of my life; spirit, soul, and body.

I am dependent upon the Word and will not be moved by those things that I think, see, hear or feel. The peace of God that flows out of His Word is great upon me, and my composure remains undisturbed, no matter what I may face in life.

Day Seven

THE PEACE OF SECURITY

"So do not fear, for I am with you; do not be dismayed, for I am your God. I will strengthen you and help you; I will uphold you with my righteous right hand."

Isaiah 41:10

As a child, the thought of somebody breaking into our home and possibly harming me never crossed my mind. I never consciously thought about the matter at all. It was not until I found myself at home alone after school one day when my mind began to lie to me, and all sorts of scenarios ran through my head. My imagination was running wild, and before I knew it, I was hiding in my bedroom closet until my mother came home. I convinced myself that evildoers were at every window and door in the house. The truth of the matter is that nobody was after me at all, nor was anybody stalking our home to break in and cause me harm. I was perfectly safe, but you could not tell that to a young boy who had an extremely vivid imagination. My sense of security was not in knowing that my parents lived there or that they would soon be home. My security came only when they were present in the house. In their absence, my fears, insecurity, and especially, my imagination were free to run wild.

Lessons Of Peace

I Will Uphold You: That is the amazing promise of this scripture. We are commanded to "fear not" based on the promise that God will always be with us. His presence alone is the basis for our security. The thief that comes to "steal, kill and destroy" knows that he is a defeated foe, and the very presence of the Lord enforces his defeat. But the "promise-source" relative to our peace continues: God declares that not only are we not to fear, but neither are we to be dismayed. Life itself offers plenty of opportunities to become distressed, discouraged, and disappointed, but God promises that the peace of His presence transcends all of the letdowns of life. *"I will strengthen you, help you and uphold you with my righteous right hand" (Isaiah 41:10).* The promise of God to uphold you means that He has a "holy grasp" on you that circumstances or issues cannot deter. God never vacillates in His commitment toward you or wavers in His ability to surround you with His peace. His peace is a "stronghold" on you. It is sustaining, never lacking, always available, and is always enough.

Psalm 18:2 (NLT) says, "The LORD is my rock, my fortress, and my Savior; my God is my rock, in whom I find protection. He is my shield, the power that saves me, and my place of safety." When you set yourself to walk in the peace of God (which is the very essence of God, Himself), that peace becomes the rock of His presence upon which you stand; it becomes your fortress of protection that the enemy cannot penetrate with His lies or deception.

Today's Confession of Peace

Lord, you are my security; you are the very presence of Peace; you are peace. It is your peace that enforces the enemy's defeat, and I choose to hide myself in your grace, your promise, and your purposes.

No matter what I face today, I am confident that your grace transcends the lies, strategies, and attempts of the enemy to separate me from your provision of peace.

I will not fear, I will not be dismayed, and neither will I be discouraged in what I see, think, hear or feel. I will not be drawn in by the enemies' deceptive practices.

I set my heart on your peace, and you strengthen me with your strong right arm. I am sheltered, protected, and hidden in the peace of God that is my stronghold. Let the winds blow, let the waves crash, I shall not be moved.

Day Eight

THE PEACE OF HIS PRESENCE

"Be strong and courageous. Do not be afraid or terrified because of them, for the Lord your God goes with you; he will never leave you nor forsake you."

Deuteronomy 31:6

In this passage, we find ourselves observing a nation that has faced incredible odds. Under the leadership of Moses, the people of Israel have witnessed God do the impossible. Amazingly, they witnessed the freedom of their nation after 430 years under the cruel bondage of Egypt. Time and again, God has proven Himself faithful to these wandering and lost people. By the strength of His right arm, He miraculously delivered them from slavery, death, oppression, and years of severe cruelty under a heartless leader. As if that were not enough, He gathered them together under the love, passion, and strength of His mighty arms as they wandered through the wilderness towards a land of peace, provision, and promise.

Lessons Of Peace

A Trusted Father: As He always does, God raised a man who served as a leader to the people of Israel. Moses was not only a prophetic voice to his people but became a trusted father who faithfully led a people who were, in fact, often faithless in their pursuit of the dream and the promise. Faced with impossible odds in the natural, Moses was the man who continually brought the children of Israel back to the heart and the hand of God. Through his leadership, they experienced the provision, protection, and presence of God in a dry, weary and dangerous land. Against personal odds, leading a hard-hearted people, enemies on every side, and harsh, unrelenting living conditions, Moses became a champion of his people. In this chapter, he now comes to the end of his life. Being the leader he is, he prepares the people for what is ahead: new leadership, new challenges, new opportunities, and even new enemies. The words that he declares over them are words of life and peace. Be strong and courageous, and do not be afraid or terrified, knowing that the God of peace will always be with you. In essence, Moses is saying that he was never the source of their peace, provision, or protection; it was always God.

Being Strong and Courageous: In his parting words, Moses specifically addressed Israel's enemies and brought instruction not be afraid because of them. His commanding instruction is to be strong. The Hebrew word for strong is "chazaq," and it means to be resolute, firm, courageous, and to prevail. That is what peace will do in your life. God's peace brings a sense of courage, strength, and resolution that you do not have to be moved by the circumstances you are facing. Knowing that Israel would see things they had never seen before, Moses is instructing them in the way of godly peace, which will sustain them regardless of what they might come up against. The promise of peace is predicated on His presence, of which they were assured as they journeyed into a land that was promised, but not yet secured. As you move into the arenas of life unfamiliar to you, the promise of His peace and His presence goes with you. He will never leave you nor forsake you.

Today's Confession of Peace

On every side, I have reasons not to be at peace. I have seen the issues of life before me that are unjust, unfair, and insecure.

I have witnessed the ravaging of the enemy in those that I love and have no confidence in my abilities or of my ability to defeat the hand of the enemy on my own accord.

However, I am thankful that my enemies have already been defeated, and I am filled with peace that passes understanding. I am resolute, firm, unmoving, and confident in the peace of God that prevails in every arena of my life.

Even when I find myself in a dry and weary land, I am confident in the protection, provision, presence, and peace of God that surrounds me on every side as a shield.

In places where I am unfamiliar, I remain confident, unshakeable, and always abiding in the presence of God that will never leave me nor forsake me.

Day Nine

THE FRUIT OF PEACE

"But the fruit of the Spirit is love, joy, peace, patience, kindness, goodness, faithfulness, gentleness, self-control. Against such, there is no law. And those who are Christ's have crucified the flesh with its passions and desires. If we all live in the Spirit, let us also walk in the Spirit. Let us not become conceited, provoking one another, envying one another."

Galatians 5:22-26

The Greek word for fruit is significant in today's passage. It is the word "karpos," meaning to "flow from." In other words, it is not that we are to go out and look for the existing "fruit of the spirit" and work to make it ours, in order for it to become a part of our "Christian repertoire." The fruit is the evident outflowing that results from being people who are filled with the Holy Spirit. Karpos means "the fruit of one's loins." In 1 Peter 1:13, we are admonished to "gird up our loins." Your "loins" are the spiritually reproductive part of who you are as a believer. The Israelites considered your loins as the very central part of who you are, from which flowed all issues relative to life. The same concept is found in Proverbs 4:23 where we are instructed to "guard our hearts."

Lessons Of Peace

The Power of Intimacy: Neither the gifts nor the fruit of the Spirit are objects that are to be "sought and seized," but the natural outflow of the relationship we have with God. The more intimate you become with the Lord, the greater the level of the gifts and the fruit you will see evident in your life. Peace is an outflow of our intimacy with the Lord. It grows out of a relationship and results from our passion for Jesus as Lord of our lives. Have you left fruit on your counter unattended? What was the result? At our house, it doesn't take long before it is spoiled and worthless and becomes something that must be dealt with.

What started as fresh, vibrant, full of life, and desirable; quickly became that which had to be thrown away. What is the point of that illustration? The peace of God (and all of the fruit of the Spirit) in your life must be guarded and protected. Fruit is only good if it is consumed within the appropriate time, so it is with peace. God longs for you to live in the fullness of His peace. His purposes are for the fruit of the Spirit to be a daily benefit in your life.

The Power of Fruit: I Corinthians 13:2 declares, "If we have all the gifts, but not love (fruit), we are as "clanging cymbals." Since we are on the subject of fruit and gifts, let us take the opportunity to "unpack that." In the Old Testament, the priestly garments were a type and shadow of the Messiah and the Church. As described in Exodus 28, the outer garment of the priest was called the cloak. At the bottom of the cloak hung golden bells and red, blue, and purple ornaments in the shape and texture of pomegranates. When the priest walked, the bells (gifts of the Spirit) between the pomegranates (fruit of the Spirit) made a musical sound. If the pomegranates had been removed, the bells would have rattled against each other, and the sound would have been harsh, unpleasant, and uninviting. So it is with our lives. Without the fruit of the Spirit, without peace, our lives become difficult, unpleasant, and uninviting.

In this same passage, we discover that there is "no law" against the fruit of the Spirit. There is nothing more significant than the fruit of the Spirit. Nothing transcends the peace of God, not even the law of sin or the law of fear. We are called to walk in God's peace even as the priest walks, wearing the cloak. We are called to guard, preserve and protect the peace of God so that our lives are inviting, pleasant, and of great value.

Today's Confession of Peace

I walk in the divine fruit of the Spirit, the spirit of peace. I am passionate and hungry for more of God, and in my pursuit of Him, I find Him and all of His attributes, including all of the fruit of the Spirit.

I will not allow the lies and deceptive practices of the enemy to cause my fruit to spoil. My life is attractive, inviting, and pleasant in all that I encounter.

I live according to God's plans and purposes for my life, which includes the fullness of the gifts and the fruit of the Spirit. I place a careful guard on my life and will not allow the peace of God to be stolen from me.

I walk in peace, and I live by peace, and my mind is settled because of the peace of God. I am fresh, vibrant, and full of life and love, and victory. Peace overflows in all that concerns me, and I am steadfast and unmovable.

Day Ten

THE SOURCE OF PEACE

"Peace I leave with you; my peace I give you. I do not give to you as the world gives. Do not let your hearts be troubled, and do not be afraid."

John 14.27

The constructs of the enemy's strategies aligned against your peace are pretty subtle and highly complex. The source of your peace is spiritual, yet the "platform" upon which it is to be realized is in the realm of your emotions. To adequately describe and discuss our emotions' intricacies and complexities is an entirely different book and quite an exhaustive one at that. The enemy of your peace is the master at weaving emotional experiences together, disrupting your peace, your stability, your perspective, and your view of yourself and others. His strategies often incorporate guilt from past decisions and actions, regret from unfulfilled dreams and promises, a fear of the future and the unknown. They can also include the heavy hand of others' opinions and attitudes from those who do not know you or even understand you. The lack of peace can also stem from unresolved conflict or situations and circumstances that never found a sense of closure.

Lessons Of Peace

The Overflow of Peace: It was in the garden of Gethsemane that Jesus stared into the cup of wrath (the lack of peace), and although every natural part of Him was repulsed by what He saw, He consented to the will of the Father to bring peace to your world. "The chastisement of our peace was laid upon Him," Isaiah 53:5. Now you know what Jesus meant when He said, "Peace, I leave with you." Your peace was bought and paid for because Jesus shed His blood for it. It is the believer's inherited right and belongs to you because you were included in the will. The enemy has no right to your peace. It belongs to you, and as it is with all of your valuable assets, it must be protected at all costs. One of the essential components in protecting peace is to realize that peace is an overflow, never a pursuit. In other words, I am in pursuit of a relationship with Jesus, and from that relationship flows the peace that reaches beyond my capacity and understanding. I cannot and will not find authentic peace outside of Jesus.

The Power of Peace: As in all things, the enemy has a substitute for the peace of God that is based upon the riches, treasures, and pursuit of worldly gain. Jesus states in this scripture that He has something to offer, but so does the world, and the choice is yours. The word "kosmos" that Jesus refers to in terms of the world, references earthly goods, riches, advantages, and pleasures. The original word in Greek also describes those things as hollow, frail, fleeting, and seductive, all obstacles to the very cause of Christ in your life. This is not about pleasure; this is about peace. Even when life's circumstances become unpleasurable, you can still maintain emotional peace when your relationship with Christ is intact.

The Protector of Peace: It is essential to note that in this scripture, he begins by defining precisely what He is offering in terms of peace. He elaborates that He alone is the source of peace, and suddenly, He shifts gears as well as focus. He makes His declaration, and then, the directive of maintaining peace is placed squarely upon the shoulders of the recipient of that peace. He says to us, His disciples, "Do not let your heart be troubled, do not let it be afraid." Wait, that means that I am the "protector of my peace." It is my choice to either stay in peace or allow the circumstances of my life to dictate my emotional status. In the middle of the Sea of Galilee, Jesus confronted His disciples with the question: "why are you afraid"?

There is always the possibility of storms arising, that things are not always going to go your way, but the promise and the command of the Lord to go to "the other side" has already been given. The time to determine that you are going to walk in peace is before the storm. The storms do not dictate my peace, my perspective, or my purpose.

God has already spoken, even as He did to Joshua before going into the Promised Land, "have I not commanded you to be strong and courageous?" Joshua 1:9.

Today's Confession of Peace

I rise today and embrace the inheritance that is mine as a believer and a follower of Jesus Christ. My stability, my perspective of life, my view of myself and others is not determined nor dictated by past failures, disappointments, regrets, or unfulfilled dreams.

I am a new creation in Christ, and I have every right to walk in the divine peace that is mine in Christ. I am not moved by others' opinions or by a fear of the unknown or of the future.

I have every confidence that He who has begun a good work in me will bring it to fruition and completion. I am established by the promise of peace that I have in my relationship with Jesus.

I walk according to His word and His heart, and I will not be moved by what I see, hear, think or feel. I will not be led astray by the storms that arise on the lake of my life. I have a promise that I will get to the other side, and today, I rise in strength and courage and a fresh and new determination to be all God has called me to be.

Day Eleven

STRENGTHENED AND ENCOURAGED

"May our Lord Jesus Christ himself and God our Father, who loved us and by his grace gave us eternal encouragement and good hope, encourage your hearts and strengthen you in every good deed and word."

2 Thessalonians 2:16-17

God loves you. Read that sentence a few times over and just let it soak into your emotional wellbeing. God loves you. He is passionate about you and has you on His mind night and day. He never stops thinking about you or looking for ways to lavish His love upon you. His Word declares that His purposes over you are yes, and amen.

The devil has convinced so many believers that God is mad at them and is ready to strike them down with a disease, sickness, or some type of calamity to punish and discipline them for their sins.

Yes, God indeed disciplines those that He loves, but His discipline is never punitive; it is always corrective. He leads and guides us in the way in which we should go. God wants you to be encouraged, and He wants you to have a sense of hope and to be strengthened in what you do, both in word and deed.

He wants to fulfill His passions and purposes in your life, and He does not fluctuate about how He feels about you. He always loves you.

Lessons Of Peace

The Love of A Father: Since this a book on peace, you might be asking yourself what this has to do with peace? When you walk in the confidence of the love of God, His peace *always* accompanies His love. If the enemy can convince you that God does not love you, he can also steal your peace and your joy, and even your faith. But God does love you, and it is important to Him that you walk in His love and peace over your life. This is not just a "theological love" or a "fatherly love"; this is "agapao." This is a love that surrounds you with favor and peace. This is a love that is passionate, not passive. This is a love that causes God to treat you with the deepest affection and tenderness. This is a love that causes God to look at you with deep fondness and contentment. The root word of agapao suggests that this is a love where God is looking for opportunities to "kiss" you and constantly show you signs of His love.

Encouraged in His Love: Because I know that my wife is deeply committed to me and loves me, I have peace in our relationship. I do not wake up every morning wondering if this is the day she will leave me. I have never even entertained those thoughts. Because we have a healthy relationship, I am secure in who I am with her and our marriage. There is no lack of peace in our home due to a relational strain or uncertainty of how we feel about one another. If situations do arise between us, we have the maturity to sit down, talk it out, learn from it and grow from there. We do not harbor bitterness or resentment against each other. We forgive, forget and move on. So it is in your relationship with the Father. You can know that He deeply and passionately loves you and wants to forgive you, not judge you. He does not hold on to your past sins or hold grudges against you. He only has thoughts of success and prosperity towards you for the future. You are awesome to Him.

Our scripture reading today tells us to be encouraged by the Father's love for us and allow His grace and peace to wash over us to strengthen us in what we say and do. So, be encouraged today. When the enemy tries to make you feel that God is mad at you or does not like you, remind him that not only does God love you and have a future and a plan for your life, but you are His favorite, and there is nothing he can do about it.

Today's Confession of Peace

I am so glad that God loves me and that He has a perfect plan for my life. I am deeply moved by His passion for me, and I set myself to rise to the purposes that He has established over my life.

Never again will I allow the enemy to lie to me or steal the joy of the Lord away from me. I will not allow my peace to be disrupted or derailed by destructive thoughts that God is anything other than passionate about me.

God's love for me and His peace over me does not fluctuate, and I am confident in His ability to surround me with all that I need to walk in peace and to abound in His love for me.

Day Twelve

TURN YOUR EYES UPON JESUS

"The Lord turn his face toward you and give you peace."

Numbers 6:26

Here we find a scripture that is so simple and yet, so profound. "May the Lord lift up His countenance upon you" (Numbers 6:26). This scripture is part of the priestly blessing that was pronounced upon the people of Israel every year on the Day of Atonement by the High Priest. The message was simple: God longs to look upon you and the result of His passionate gaze is His peace and His presence. In his greatest time of need, King David sought the Lord that He might cause His face to "shine upon him". David knew and understood that the countenance of God upon Him was one of favor and grace. It was a look of love and literally means that your "face is lit up with a smile". Every parent knows that look. It is a sense of great pleasure in your child, simply because he or she is your child. They haven't necessarily done anything to earn it, and may not even technically deserve it, but hey, they are your kids and that is enough. It is not always a look or a love that can be articulated, but it is strong, it is real, and it is lasting.

Lessons Of Peace

The Look of Salvation: David knew that it was literally a "look of salvation" and that it would result in deliverance because of the mercy of God. The mercy of God "chesed" is also translated as loving-kindness, steadfast love, compassion, and always implies the peace, the love and the grace of God that is based on His covenantal promises. "May the Chesed of your countenance, your salvation (yeshu'ah) always be turned towards me." Invoking the Lord's countenance upon us is not a prayer, but a proclamation. It is a declaration of my faith that as I have surrendered my life to Christ, His gaze is never broken from me.

The countenance of God upon me is His promise that He not only notices me, but that He is acutely aware of the affairs of my life, and that as my Father, He is engaged in my daily activities, and I am the recipient of His favor. His favor is upon my life, my circumstances and my conditions, and He approves of my life and fills me with His peace.

This is the Day: God's countenance is that of a powerful, wise and omnipotent Being. His is a countenance of exuberant gladness, overflowing joy and fills your soul with peace and gladness. "This is the day that the Lord has made, I will rejoice and be glad in it" (Psalm 118:24). That day is the day of salvation. There is no greater expression of the love and light of God than that of our salvation, which has come through Jesus Christ. Daily, the light of His countenance shines upon us and the hand of His love rests heavily upon us. We were lost in confusion, chaos and darkness and the light of His love has brought us into peace, love and fellowship with the Father. I can live my life knowing that God's countenance and His peace is continually upon me because of Christ. I am never alone; I am never forsaken, and I am never lost. I walk in the confidence of His countenance and the fact that He never takes His eyes off of me.

Today's Confession of Peace

I was lost, but now I am found. I was blind, but now I see. There was a time in my life when I groped around in the darkness, with no sense of direction, no peace and no confidence in life.

Jesus changed all of that. Thank you, Lord that out of your love for me, you redeemed my life, turned your countenance upon me and filled my life to overflowing with the life, love and peace of whom you are. Thank you for causing your face to shine upon me and lifting your countenance towards me. As your child, I walk in your steadfast love, your loving kindness, your eternal patience and grace and am the recipient of your favor and your mercy.

Thank you for blessing me, keeping me, and causing your face to shine upon me, for being gracious to me, lifting your countenance upon me and giving me your peace.

Day Thirteen

THE LINES ARE DRAWN

*"Lord, you have assigned me my portion and my cup; you have
made my lot secure. The boundary lines have fallen for me in
pleasant places; surely, I have a delightful inheritance. I will praise
the Lord, who counsels me; even at night my heart instructs me. I
have set the Lord always before me. Because he is at my right hand,
I will not be shaken."*

Psalm 16:5-8

My life is not up for grabs. I am a person under divine assignment
and supernatural appointment. I live under the watchful eye of my
Father and He secures the borders of my life. He is my strong tower
and the mighty fortress of who I am and who I am becoming. He is
my peacemaker and the One who leads me in pleasant places. Our
scripture reading today describes God as my "cup." The Hebrew
word is "Kos" and it means that He is the one who holds me all
together. The human mentality is to always look out for number one,
but here we find that God is actually looking out for you in all
things. That produces a feeling of confident peace that nothing else
can. This is not about you "figuring it all out" and "getting it all
together;" this is about you living a life of peaceful surrender to the
Father who knows how to take care of you and longs to do so.

Lessons Of Peace

The Pleasant Places: As a father, I have taught my children that there is a difference between being rich and being wealthy. To be wealthy means to have great possessions and to be abundantly supplied with resources. To be rich means to possess something of great value and great worth. In life, you may not necessarily be monetarily wealthy, but you can rest assured that you are rich in God. You are guaranteed an inheritance and a heritage, and the Word declares over you that the boundary lines concerning your life have fallen in "pleasant places". God has measured life in your favor. He has given you more than you will ever need to be a success in life and to walk in the peace, the authority, the grace and the favor of your Father in every arena of your life.

The Power of Prophetic Praise: The effect of His favor upon your life is that you are one who rises to bless Him in all that you do and in who you are. Your lips will continually praise Him, your heart will rejoice before Him, your soul will be glad and delight in the God of your salvation. Regardless of what you see in the realm of the natural, you will not be moved by the demonic strategies of the enemy, but by your prophetic praise. You will bring circumstances and issues into divine alignment with God's declared word over you, by virtue of His intended plan for your life.

Even in the "night watches" your emotions and affections are at peace because you rest in your portion and your inheritance, which is peace. There are times when I wake up in the night and have a difficult time going back to sleep because my mind is racing a hundred miles per hour. Admittedly, there are some nights; I lie in bed, in the darkness of the night, and the tormenting lies of the enemy come against me.

Once I open the door to those lies, my imagination begins to take over, which is never good. In those times I must stand on the promise of my inheritance. By the Word, I come to the place where my emotions are at peace and my mind instructs me in the ways of God whether I am asleep or awake. I love the fact that the saturation overflow of His Word impacts me even when I am not consciously aware of it.

Today's Confession of Peace

I walk in the divine and supernatural appointment of the Lord. My life is unique, and I am a special creation of God. I was born for such a time as this.

I am not a mistake, nor am I simply the biological result of my parent's relationship. I was fearfully and wonderfully crafted by the hand of the Lord and knit together in my mother's womb.

My heavenly Father watches over me, surrounds me with His peace and His favor and is the One that holds my life together. Because of His great love over me, I walk in confidence and in peace and rest in the inheritance that is mine in Him.

God's favor rests upon me and the blessing of His life on me is my portion and my lot. I will not be moved by demonic strategies but rise with a prophetic praise on my lips as I enjoy the saturation overflow that permeates every part of who I am.

Day Fourteen

THE BLESSING OF PEACE

"The Lord gives his people strength. The Lord blesses them with peace."

Psalm 29:11

If you get nothing else from this book, I pray that you get this: "peace is not an emotion." Emotions are fickle and can deceive you. Your feelings can change on a whim and are subject to diverse and varied circumstances. The dictionary defines emotion as "a natural instinctive state of mind deriving from one's circumstances, mood, or relationships with others." Emotions can be hyped up, driven, manipulated, and are pretty subjective.

On the other hand, peace is a "state of being" and the result of a heart of surrender to the Prince of Peace. This is true peace from God, and in this God-Peace, we find strength, sustenance, and power. Yes, there is *power* in peace. Power to stay the course regardless of the circumstances and power to maintain a "presence of mind" when all of the "facts" are nothing more than confusing.

Lessons Of Peace

Perfect Peace: The power of God's peace accelerates you beyond the scope and the demands of the circumstances at hand and postures you to be able to respond out of a state of tranquility as opposed to reacting from the pressure cooker of raw emotions. The strength that the Psalmist is referring to is your emotional, mental and physical state of being. When you are operating in God's peace, you find the ability and anointing to clearly articulate the heart and mind of God. However, not only will you be able to articulate the mind of God, you will be able to discern His plans and purposes despite the raging storm around you.

That is precisely what happened when Jesus was asleep in the boat, and a storm came up in the middle of the Sea of Galilee. He was already at perfect peace, exercising the ability to rest even in the middle of a storm, and from that place of strength and peace, He rebuked the wind and spoke peace to the waves. Please do not miss this important principle: it is FROM a place of peace that we are able to declare peace.

His emotions never got the best of Him, His mind was able to discern the storm, and out of the strength of peace, He dictated the perfect will of God into the realm of the natural. You will never do that as long as you are in a place of fear, torment, and turmoil.

The Blessing of Peace: Peace is not only the power of God activated in your life; it is also the blessing of God released in your life. As we have already learned, the pronouncement of God's shalom upon the people of God was significant in the Old Testament, even as it is in today's Jewish culture. God's blessing means that you are anointed to win, empowered to prosper, impossible to curse. You cannot win if you are not at peace, and you will find it difficult to thrive if there is a lack of peace in your life. The lack of peace is located within the curse. You are blessed with peace. It is inherent in your DNA as a believer. It is God's promise over you, and you have every right to stand in faith and enforce the peace of God in your life, your family, and your circumstances.

Today's Confession of Peace

I am not tossed around by my emotions. I am a person of stability and peace, regardless of any turbulence in my world. Today, I surrender my heart afresh to the Prince of Peace and declare Him as Lord over all that concerns me.

He is Lord of my past, and I will not allow the whispers, lies, or suggestions of the past to dictate or determine who I am or how I live. I will stay the course, I will be focused, and I will be unshakeable, unmovable, and always abounding in the supernatural peace of God.

Because of God's peace, I possess the ability to discern God's plans and purposes, even amid the storms that come up in my life.

The presence of a storm does not determine the peace that I walk in. From that place of peace, I declare God's will, decree His purposes and call into manifestation His perfect peace.

I am anointed to win, empowered to prosper, and impossible to curse because of that peace.

Day Fifteen

FEAR OR PEACE, YOU CHOOSE

"The Lord is my light and my salvation – whom shall I fear? The Lord is the stronghold of my life – of whom shall I be afraid?"

Psalm 27:1

Peace has many enemies, but one of the greatest enemies of peace is fear. Once you give in to fear, the effects of it are paralyzing. It will affect you physically, spiritually, and emotionally and lead to instability, unhappiness, and discontentment. Fear will drain you of your spiritual life and sap you of vision, perspective and confidence. Fear will separate you from God and His blessing and provision.

Lessons Of Peace

The Personal Prophetic Declaration: The Psalmist makes a strong prophetic declaration over himself relative to his place in God and God's place in him. In faith he declares: "The Lord is my light and my salvation." He is not in a moment of panic or distress when he makes his declaration but is covering his day in faith. He has learned that the best time to make your stand in faith is *before* things fall apart. Please do not miss the fact that this is not just the "mutterings of a psalmist;" it is a decree of God's life in him. As he states that God is his light and salvation, he is engaging the benefits of his salvation, which is the Hebrew word, "Yesha." It means deliverance, rescue, safety, and welfare; in other words, the peace of God.

Whom Shall I Fear: All of a sudden, the Psalmist turns his declaration away from who God is and begins to make a declaration over himself and his own life. He asks the question, "whom shall I fear?" How he sees God in His life determines how he sees himself. Because God is my light and my salvation, I am walking in supernatural deliverance, safety, welfare, and redemption. I will NOT walk in fear but peace. To do justice to this scripture, we have to take a quick look at the original meaning for fear.

The Hebrew word is "yare," and it means to be dreadful, to be fearful, to be astonished and terrified. Please notice that each of those words deal with the realm of your emotions, where fear strikes you. Peace is always more significant and substantial than fear, and the fact that God is your light and your salvation gives you the biblical and legal right to live in peace.

The Safety of Peace: As we relate peace to this scripture, we come to a new understanding of how strong the power of peace is. The God of peace is my "stronghold" and "the strength" of my life. He is my place of safety, my protection, and my refuge. Peace is my safety. I am protected by peace and I find refuge in the peace of God. Those words describe the protective covering of peace. When you look at the Psalmist relationship with God, it becomes apparent that you gain peace through intimacy with Him. Through a personal and intimate relationship, the Psalmist has discovered God to be his light, salvation, and stronghold. His understanding of God, and his faith confession concerning God, produces peace in his life. Through peace, I find a firm foundation, and through peace I prevail in my life.

Today's Confession of Peace

I stand against the enemy of my peace. I will not make room, compromise, or tolerate any level of fear in my life. I am not a person that is given to fear, and I have no place in my life for fear.

I walk in divine health and wholeness: physically, emotionally, and spiritually, and I am a person of divine and supernatural peace.

I will not be separated from God or His blessing and provision. Even as the Psalmist declared over his life, I declare that God is my light and He is my salvation, and based on that,
I will fear nothing or no one.

As the redeemed of God, I walk in the power and peace of my salvation, deliverance, safety, and welfare. My emotions are stable, and I stand against dread, ungodly astonishment, and terror.

I have a biblical and legal right to live a life of supernatural peace. When the storms of life rage against me, the God of peace is my place of protection, He is my safety, refuge, and covering. I walk in intimacy with Him, and I stand on a firm foundation from which I prevail in peace.

Day Sixteen

BE ANXIOUS FOR NOTHING

"Do not be anxious about anything, but in every situation, by prayer and petition, with thanksgiving, present your requests to God. And the peace of God, which transcends all understanding, will guard your hearts and your minds in Christ Jesus."

Philippians 4:6-7

We live in an anxious world. You can look around our world and easily find troubles, cares, concerns, and trials. The news media consistently reports of turmoil worldwide, and there is never a lack of a new threat. There is always a new disaster or crisis that we could quickly become worried about if we chose to. We have financial crisis reports, medical concerns, social unrest, and political turmoil; the list is endless. And in the face of all of that, the Bible tells us not to be anxious about "anything." Wow. Is that burying our head in the sand or being irresponsible about what is going on around us? Should not we be concerned about our children, our families, and our futures?

Lessons of Peace

Don't Be Anxious: This is not a flippant scripture that encourages us to ignore the issues in life around us, but a biblical directive and mandate complete with a divine strategy to walk in peace. The word anxious carries the connotation of being troubled with care, being burdened with anxiety, and being "separated into factions." What does that mean? The Bible tells us not to be double-minded, and that is what anxiousness and anxiety does. It separates you emotionally from the peace of God and creates confusion and chaos in your soul. You love God and trust Him, and you want to follow His heart, but when anxiety sets in, the overwhelming sense of fear, dread, and terror stops you in your tracks and robs you of your faith and your peace.

Prayer, Thanksgiving, and Surrender: The three-fold strategy as outlined in this scripture is relatively non-complex. It involves prayer, thanksgiving, and surrender. We all face turmoil in our lives and giants and mountains that are bigger than we are, but often, we wait until the situation becomes unbearable before we cry out to God. At that point, we are crying out in desperation, fighting anxiety and struggling for relief and resolve.

Having a strategy before facing those issues is the point of today's time in the Word. In every situation, commit to being a person of prayer. That means refusing to leave the problem up for grabs but instead covering it in prayer and bringing it to the One who already has absolute power, dominion, and authority over it. This is a great place to remind you that prayer is not begging and pleading God to do something on your behalf, but rising in faith, declaration, and decreeing what He has already promised you in His Word.

Living A Life of Praise: The second aspect of the peace strategy outlined by the Apostle Paul is that of living a life of praise. I once heard somebody mistakenly say, "the Bible says that we are to praise God for everything we go through in life." 1 Thessalonians 5:18 tells us that we are to "give thanks to God "in" all things; meaning that during times of crisis, we must continue to be a people of worship. Whatever or whomever you worship becomes exalted and magnified in your life. When you worship and praise God during difficult times, He becomes more significant than whatever it is that you are facing.

We need to stop telling God how big our mountains are and start telling our mountains how big our God is! Worship is eternal, and it not only elevates you above the trials you are facing but gives you a perspective that allows you to see beyond the moment. Worship strengthens your inner man and supernaturally connects you to the God of peace, allowing you to live as a person who responds to a crisis as opposed to reacting to it.

The Power of Surrender: Finally, the third step in this strategy is that of surrender. Presenting your requests to God is an act of humbly submitting to His desires and purposes and acknowledging that He has all dominion and authority, and a Name that is above every name, Philippians 2:9-11. That acknowledgment is an aspect of our relationship with Him. Proverbs 3:5-6 says, "Trust in the LORD with all your heart, and lean not on your understanding; in all your ways acknowledge Him, and He shall direct your paths." The word "acknowledge" is the Hebrew word "Yada," and it is the Jewish idiom for an intimate relationship between a man and a woman.

That is the level of intimacy and surrender to which God is calling us as His children. It is in that place that you have a "knowing" that whatever you are walking through is under the complete command of the One who loves you with deep and intimate love. That is a good feeling, and that is a safe place.

The Posture of Peace: When you posture yourself before the Lord in prayer, worship, and surrender, the result is always the peace of God. It is a peace that transcends or surpasses our "understanding," which means our thoughts, feelings, purposes, and desires. When you are walking through a personal crisis, the battleground is your mind. Your thoughts and emotions become skewed, and your senses and desires begin to shift towards that which is ungodly and unbiblical. The peace of God transcends your feelings and becomes a protective barrier from the onslaught of the enemy and a place where you can live above the fray of the battle.

Today's Confession of Peace

Even though I live in a world filled with chaos, confusion, turmoil, and anxiety, I confess that I will not be moved. I am anchored in the peace of God, and my life is not up for grabs.

I will not be tossed on the winds of the lies of the enemy, and I will not come out of a place of peace. I am steady and consistent. I am living a life that is dictated and governed by the Word of God, and His Word is my daily guide, my protection, and the source of my peace.

I am not moved by what I see, hear, think or feel, but only by what God says about me and who He says I am. I commit to a life of prayer, worship, and surrender, and come before the One who is the Lord over all that is.

I have the confidence, conviction, and courage that I am covered and protected from all of the lies and strategies of the enemy and that the peace of God surrounds me at a level that transcends my thoughts, feelings, purposes, and desires. I will not be a person who complains to God about how big my mountain is, but I will shout grace to my mountain and declare to it how big my God is.

Day Seventeen

THE POWER OF PEACE

"For God has not given us a spirit of fear and timidity, but of power, love, and sound mind."

2 Timothy 1:7

God is a giver of good gifts. I always find it amazing when bad things happen in life, and the first thing people ask is, "why did God do that?" Let it be known that God is not capable of evil, and He does not use tools out of the enemy's toolbox to accomplish His will and His purposes in your life. If you are caught up in the schemes and strategies of the enemy, God will redeem them on your behalf, but He never engages the enemy to do His will when it comes to His children. In this scripture, the Apostle Paul is teaching foundational truth to a young leader. We will do well to embrace the reality of this teaching. Fear and intimidation never find their source in God.

God Is Power: God does not "possess" power; He is power. Power finds its source in Him. He does not "possess" love; He is love. Love finds its origin in Him. God does not "possess" peace; He is peace. Peace finds its source in Him. People, who have an unhealthy fear of God, never find his love, power, or peace. Believers who never learn to walk in soundness of mind (a biblical understanding and perspective) will never unlock the true riches of the love, power, and peace of God but will become susceptible to the spirit of fear and timidity. The result of fear is always timidity, but the product of peace is always boldness and confidence. As has already been stated in this book, fear and intimidation will keep you from living in the peace, love, and authority of God.

The Peace of a Sound Mind: A "sound mind" is to have a mind that is not tossed about by a plethora of emotions. A sound mind is not divided, tormented, confused, or out of control; but at peace. The enemy's strategy is to grip your mind and emotions with great fear. Our minds and imagination are powerful; and can easily create scenarios that are not even real but seem to be.

I know of people that have convinced themselves of their defeat, even before the battle begins. When you walk in the confidence of mind that God has already redeemed any situation on your behalf, you can rise in faith, conviction, and peace regardless of how things appear in the natural. God has invested resources in you, and everything that you need to be a success in life is already on the inside of you. You have been anointed with power, you are anchored in love, and you have the mind of Christ. Great peace is upon you, and your composure is undisturbed.

Today's Confession of Peace

I thank you, Father, that you care enough for me always to give your very best. I am so glad that you are not mad at me; you do not want to judge me, but you have an everlasting love for me. You want to forgive me, restore me, and redeem my life with all good things.

You are always a good, good God and are not capable of causing me harm or injury. You never use the tools of the enemy to bring instruction or correction into my life.

I will not walk in fear or intimidation at any level, but I only walk in faith, power, love, and soundness of mind. I am not moved by what I see, think, hear or feel, but only by God's word over me.

My emotions are at peace, and I am not a person given to a spirit that is anything less than that of love, peace, and power. Everything that I need to succeed in life is already inside me, the anointing of power, love, and peace. That is Jesus.

Day Eighteen

PEACE, A WORK OF REDEMPTION

"Therefore, since we have been made right in God's sight by faith, we have peace with God because of what Jesus Christ our Lord has done for us."

Romans 5:1

In my book, "Thirty-One Days of Healing," we discovered that the accomplishments of Jesus resulted from his sacrificial shedding of blood in three different places, at three different times for three different reasons. Jesus shed His blood in the garden for the redemptive right of our emotional well-being, which includes our peace, at the scourging post for the redemptive right of our physical healing and on the cross for the redemptive right of our spiritual salvation. What does that mean to you and me as believers? It means that redemption is total salvation for total man; spirit, soul, and body.

If the enemy is harassing you with turmoil, anxiety, and despair, he is attacking your God-given redemptive right to walk in peace. I have heard people say, "well, I am just going through an emotional time right now." They say that because they do not understand that the attack they are under is a direct assault on the accomplishments of Jesus in your life. Peace is not a reward for doing everything correctly in your life; it is a redemptive right that has been purchased at a very high price, the precious blood of Jesus. To see it as anything less is to undervalue and disregard not only the importance of the blood but its effect on you as a child of God.

Lessons of Peace

Justified By Faith: The literal Greek rendering of our scripture today reads like this: "Therefore, being justified by faith, we have peace with God through our Lord, Jesus Christ." This is an essential scripture for every believer who is seeking to walk in supernatural peace. According to this scripture, peace is a direct result of our justification by faith. When you embrace salvation by faith, you embrace peace. When you embrace your healing by faith, you embrace peace. Justification is the process of a complete work of regeneration. There has been a change of persons. You were once in the dark, and now you are in the light. As an unjustified or un-regenerated person, you lived in darkness and fear, but as a believer, you live in the light and peace by justification.

The Free Gift of Salvation: It is important to remember that justification (being made whole and complete before God) results from the blood of Jesus. In other words, you didn't earn peace, you cannot manufacture peace, and you cannot counterfeit it. It is a gift of salvation, given only by God through Jesus Christ. Peace is an aspect of being righteous, innocent, faultless, and guiltless, which is the meaning of "dikaios," the Greek word for justification—what a powerful image. Being given a crown of solid gold is an amazing gift, but to be given a crown of gold that is laden with precious jewels is beyond imagination. That illustration is appropriate for this scripture. We have been given a precious, golden gift of salvation that is packaged with the precious jewel of peace.

This scripture says that we have peace with God. The word "with" is a preposition that can be interchanged with two other words, before and of. So, technically, we have peace with God, we have peace before God, and we have the peace of God. I am in a right relationship with God by peace, I can come into His presence because of peace, and I can live my life in confidence and conviction based on the peace of God in my life.

Faith is my conviction that what God has said in His word is accurate and that He will bring it to fruition. My faith engages the peace of God to operate within the context of my thoughts and brings it into reality whenever I am encountering demonic or worldly opposition in my life. I no longer have to be tossed around by the devil, but I can stand in the redemptive peace of God.

Today's Confession of Peace

Peace is not a side effect of salvation; it is salvation. The blood of Jesus redeems me, and He died for me that I might have peace. The price that He paid is too high for me not to recognize and acknowledge His goodness and His grace.

I choose to walk in every aspect of my salvation: spirit, soul, and body. I am emotionally whole and healthy. I am physically healed and healthy, and I am spiritually redeemed. I have a redemptive right to walk in peace.

The blood of Jesus has regenerated me, and I no longer live in darkness but in His marvelous light of grace and faith. God, through Jesus, makes me righteous, innocent, faultless, guiltless, and justified.

I now wear a crown of righteousness, that is adorned with the jewel of peace.

Day Nineteen

PEACE, A WORK OF THE SPIRIT

"May the God of hope fill you all with joy and peace in believing so that by the power of the Holy Spirit, you may abound in hope."

Romans 15:13

Our God is a God of abundance, joy, and peace. He is the God of all hope. This is not a hope that is "hoping and wishing;" this hope is a confident expectancy. When people that I trust make a promise to me, it produces a joy in my heart that results from a confident expectancy. I do not doubt that they will honor their word and fulfill what they promised. That is our God. He is not a man that He should lie, but He will always accomplish what He has promised. It may not happen within your timetable, but it WILL happen.

Lessons of Peace

The God of Covenant: God is a God of covenant peace, covenant joy, and covenant abundance. He is holding nothing back from you, and His desire is for you to live a life of overcoming abundance and overflow. To abound in God is to live an "abundantly furnished" life and overflowing in measure. The Greek word for abound is "perisseuo," which means to "furnish one so richly that he has an abundance and abounds with overflow." As you think of that, I want you to think of the peace of God. The desire of the Father for His children is that we live in an overflow and abundance of peace. He longs to furnish your life so richly with peace that you have an abundance of it. Does that sound like the life you desire to live?

Holy Spirit Peace: Quite often, when we read about the power of the Holy Spirit, we naturally think about the supernatural gifts of the Spirit, particularly relative to the miraculous gifts of healing. In this scripture, the Apostle Paul says that the Holy Spirit wants to fill you with His power, with an overflowing peace and confident expectancy because of that peace.

That is further confirmation that peace is not an emotion but a very distinct and accomplished work of the Holy Spirit in your life. It comes from a life of surrender and one of confident expectancy. It looks like this: no matter what I may encounter in my life, no matter how large the mountain may loom over me, no matter how dark the night might become, I can know that by the power of the Holy Spirit, I am going to walk in a supernatural peace that cannot be stolen or taken away by any other power or entity.

The Grace of Peace: So, peace, then, is a work of the Holy Spirit; it is also a result of the work of God's grace in your life. How do you appropriate any of the gifts of the Spirit in your life? Always by faith. Paul said, "may the God of hope fill you with all joy and peace *in believing*." That phrase is "en Pistis," and it means by faith. In other words, may you be filled with joy and peace by faith. As you stand in a conviction for all that is yours in God, know that peace is

His plan and His purpose, believe for it, receive it, walk in it and allow it to overflow your life with abundance.

Today's Confession of Peace

Today, I worship you as a God of abundance. I lift my voice of praise unto you that you love me with an everlasting love and that your intention for me is abundance, joy, and peace.

You are a covenant God, and you always keep your promises, even throughout the generations. You are not a man you should lie, but your word is as pure gold, tried and tested in the furnace.

Today, I choose to live a life that is abundantly furnished and overflowing in measure. I will be filled today. I will be filled with life, health, grace, and peace. I surrender to peace.

No matter how large my mountain is or how dark my night might become, I choose peace. Peace is His plan for me; I believe it, I receive it, I walk in it, and I allow it to overflow in my life.

Day Twenty

THE HIGH PRICE OF PEACE

"But He was wounded for our transgressions; He was bruised for our iniquities; The chastisement for our peace was upon Him, And by His stripes, we are healed."

Isaiah 53:5

It is important to remember that the redemptive price that Jesus paid for our salvation encompasses the totality of man; spirit, soul, and body. In this verse, the reality of the power of redemption is revealed. He was wounded and bruised for our transgressions and iniquities (that is, the price paid for our sin), he was chastised (received correction by punishment) for the sake of our peace, and severely beaten for our physical healing. What does that mean for us as believers? To the same degree that you would never accept the lie that you are going to hell, neither should you accept the lie that you are destined to walk in anything other than the peace of God and physical health.

Lessons of Peace

Chastised for our Peace: To be chastised means to be corrected. Chastisement was laid upon the Savior, meaning that something was being corrected. What was that? It was the fact that the enemy had free and full access to our state of well-being, and we were subject to slavery. Hebrews 2:15; "and release those who through fear of death were all their lifetime subject to bondage. Before your salvation, you were a slave. Slaves are people who do what they are told. They are not free to live life with redemptive privileges, walk in terms of authority, or even express their opinions.

Because of the brutality of cruel masters, slaves lived their lives in fear and bondage. It was not just their physical bodies that were held in shackles and chains, but their mind, will, and emotions as well. Fear was the rule of the day, and any thoughts of achieving real and lasting peace were nothing more than a pipe dream.

There's a New Sheriff in Town: By the shedding of his blood, Jesus broke the power of the enemy's lies. He broke the power of sin and death and canceled the curse of the law. There is a new Sheriff in town, and fear no longer has power or authority over you. Anxiety, depression, rejection, worthlessness, and anxiousness are under the redemptive and corrective blood of Jesus. Those are the enemy tools that he uses to attempt to bring you back into the very bondage that Christ redeemed you from.

It is easy to see them as nothing more than emotions that are subject to our lives' circumstantial issues. While that certainly is how they manifest, the root goes a lot deeper than that, and the objective is a lot more insidious than that. If the enemy can get you into emotional turmoil, he can separate you from the peace of God and gain a stronghold that is difficult to break. This is not just an emotional battle; this is a spiritual battle, and the stakes are high. Jesus paid too high of a price for you to live in the bondage of Satan.

Your Legal Right to Peace: The initial key to victory is to realize that you have a legal and spiritual right to be emotionally healthy. The basis upon which you stand against the lies of the enemy that work against your peace is your knowledge and understanding of the Word, your submission to His Word, and your corresponding confession of faith. Your peace is not up for grabs. When the enemy comes against you with his schemes and strategies, stand on the Word; read it, meditate on it, memorize it, quote it, declare it, and decree it. Charge the atmosphere with your declaration of the Word over your life and your emotions. Jesus is not only Lord of your spirit, but He is also Lord over your emotions, and He is the God of all peace.

Today's Confession of Peace

I am the redeemed of God. I walk in the redemptive right of health, healing, wholeness, spirit, soul, and body. Out of His great love for me, Jesus paid the ultimate price that I might live the life of salvation.

His plan for me is not distress, turmoil, fear, or anxiety. His plan for me is perfect peace. I am at peace with God. He loves me, He accepts me, and He has a plan for my life and my future. I will not accept the enemy's lie that I have to live in anything other than peace.

I am no longer a slave. I do not live under the cruel and tormenting hand of the enemy, and He is no longer my taskmaster. My emotions do not control me, and I do not stand in a place of turmoil or torment, regardless of my circumstances.

I declare the Word of peace over my life and my family. I have a future dictated by peace, covered in peace, and my expectancy is that I will walk in the strength and power of the God of peace in all that I put my hand to.

Day Twenty-One

THE PEACE OF TRUST

"Do not let your hearts be troubled. Trust in God; trust also in me.
In my Father's house are many rooms; if it were not so, I would
have told you. I am going there to prepare a place for you. And if I
go and prepare a place for you, I will come back and take you to be
with me that you also may be where I am."

John 14:1-3

Out of the depth of your heart flow all of the issues concerning your life. The Jewish culture considered the heart to be the central "seat" of man, or literally, the "fountain" of man. From it, your emotions, desires, longings, dreams, and visions emanate. Your heart is the center of your physical being, dictating the vigor and sense of physical life, as well as the center of your spiritual life. Your heart determines your will, your character and affects your purposes and your endeavors as well as your thoughts. Your heart and your soul are the same things. It is your mind: in terms of your thought processes and how your think; it is your will: your appetites, desires, passions, and sensibilities. Your heart is also your emotions. The condition of your heart will affect your feelings, your moods, and your sentiments, as well as your relationships with others.

Lessons of Peace

No Longer Tormented: Now you know why your heart is constantly under attack. If the enemy can cause your heart to become compromised, isolated, or discouraged, he can essentially affect all that concerns your life. Proverbs 18:14, "The spirit of a man will sustain him in sickness, but who can bear a broken spirit?" In other words, your spiritual strength and stamina can see you through times of physical ailment. Still, once your spirit (your heart) becomes broken, healing becomes more difficult because it involves your mind, your will, and your emotions. At all costs, we must guard against allowing our hearts to become troubled.

To fully understand the implications of this scripture, we have to do a study on the word "troubled." It is the Greek word "tarasso" and has quite an in-depth definition. Tarasso means to be agitated or troubled, to cause an inward commotion, steal your calmness, disturb your spirit, make restless, and strike with fear or dread. It also means to render anxious, to bring perplexity or distress to mind.

When you understand that the enemy's primary target is your heart (mind, will, and emotions), it brings greater clarity and understanding to John 10:10, "the thief comes to steal, kill and destroy." If he can "trouble my heart,"; he will then possess the ability to steal my joy, kill my vision and destroy my godly passions.

Proverbs 4:23, "*Above all else*, guard your heart, for everything you do flows from it." I must fight and stand against his schemes, strategies, and tactics.

Your Trust is your Confidence: That is precisely what today's scripture is all about: how to guard your heart and stay in a place of peace so the wiles of the enemy cannot touch you. How? Trust in God. It comes back to the place of your faith. Your trust is your persuasion and your confidence. It is the place that you have come to in your relationship with Christ. It goes beyond an intellectual faith or a mere acknowledgment of His existence.

Your trust is the result of an intimate relationship with Christ that began when you made a personal commitment to His Lordship in your life. At the point that you said yes to Jesus, you started a journey of walking with Him through the highs and lows of your life. You opened your heart to His love and His Word, and He began to shape and fashion you according to His purposes. You allowed the seed of His life to take root in your spirit and your heart. The transformation began to take place and is still in effect today.

Confidence Is Established: When you said yes to Jesus, the blinders fell from your eyes, the dark shroud was lifted from your mind, and the hardness of your heart was softened to the love, grace, and mercy of God. The result is that your faith (your trust and confidence) is established in the Lord and His Word. God has declared specific promises over you that you can believe and act upon. That is how faith works. When your heart is attacked, when your peace is under siege, the promises of God rise in your heart and bring a sense of confidence regardless of what you are facing. God has a plan and a purpose that will cover you even during the darkest of trials.

So, do not "let" your heart become troubled. Stay in a place of peace, calm, and confidence by staying in the Word. Saturate your mind with the Word, cover your day with the Word, declare the Word in faith, and know that God not only has peace and a purpose for your life, but He also has a place for you. It is the place of His presence. The Word declares that in His presence is the fullness of joy. Psalm 16:11, "You make known to me the path of life, you will fill me with joy in your presence, with eternal pleasures at your right hand."

In His presence is the fullness of joy, peace, and of life. His presence is the very breath that He breathed into Adam at creation. It is the Hebrew word, "Chayah," and it means to be made alive by the very presence of God, which is the presence of blessing, of health, wholeness, prosperity, to be free from sickness, discouragement, and the snares of death. That is the place to which God has called you. That is the place of your trust and your confidence in His Word. He has promised, and He is always faithful to keep His promises because He is a covenant-keeping God.

He has a place secured for you in eternity, but He also has a place of peace, life, blessing, and prosperity here in the world in which you live right now. The enemy wants to agitate you with his lies, he wants to discourage you with reminders of your past failures, he wants to rob you of your future, but God says that you have hope and a future. Jeremiah 29:11, "For I know the plans that I have for you," declares the Lord, "plans to prosper you and not to harm you, plans to give you a hope and a future."

Today's Confession of Peace

By faith, I bring my emotions, desires, longings, dreams, and visions under the Lordship of Jesus. I have made him the Lord of my life and my heart and declare that my will, character, purposes, and endeavors are fully submitted to His perfect plan and will for my life and all that concerns me.

I place the guard of the Word over the gates of my heart: what I see, think, hear and feel, and I refuse to allow the enemy to bring me to the place where I am agitated, troubled, disturbed, or restless. I will not open the door to his lies of fear or dread.

I stand on the truth of what God says about me, and I am persuaded and confident that the same work that He has begun in me will bring to fullness and completion.

I operate in the love of God, and He is shaping and fashioning me according to His plans and purposes. The very thing that the enemy meant for my harm, God will use for my growth, maturity, and benefit.

I walk in the blessing of peace, the fulfillment of joy, and the place of confidence that His breath of health, healing, and wholeness, spirit, soul, and body has been breathed upon me in abundance.

Day Twenty-Two

CAST YOUR CARES

"Cast your burden on the Lord, and he shall sustain you: he shall never suffer the righteous to be moved."

Psalms 55:22

Walking and living in the sovereign peace of God never comes automatically. In the same way that God's will does not "just happen," there are times when you must contend for the peace of God in your life. There are seasons when you have to rise in faith and stand against the enemy's strategies that have been designed and released against you to steal your peace and joy. You have to be on guard and protect your peace continually.

Lessons of Peace

Crossing the Border: Whenever you enter into a new country, you have to cross borders. Inevitably, at these borders, you will find guards (most likely military) who secure the borders. In securing the borders, they are doing much more than just keeping non-citizens or unauthorized personnel from entering their country. They are protecting the peace of that country. They preserve the country's stability against intruders who would desire to do them harm and provide a sense of peace to the citizens. The guards are a presence against those intruders. What and who are the intruders that would attempt to cross the borders of your heart, life, and family to do you harm? The enemy of your soul has an endless cadre of lies, strategies, and weapons designed to discourage you, steal your joy, and rob your peace.

God Will make a Way: One of the enemy's subtle tricks is to convince God's people that we are destined to carry our burdens. I have heard people misquote the scripture found in 1 Corinthians 10:13, "No temptation has overtaken you except such as is common to man; but God *is* faithful, who will not allow you to be tempted beyond what you are able, but with the temptation will also make the way of escape, that you may be able to bear *it.*" This scripture is teaching us that with every temptation, God will always make a way of escape, yet I have heard people use it to indicate, "God will only give you the burdens that He knows you can bear." That is nonsense. Matthew 11:30, "For my yoke is easy, and my burden is light."

You are not supposed to carry the burdens of your life, you are supposed to cast them upon the Lord, and when you do, He promises that He will sustain you. The word "burden" in this scripture means to literally "have something laid upon you." Animals that carry heavy loads are called "beasts of burden." They are laden down with heavy loads to keep their master from having to carry it. As a child of God, you are not destined to be a "beast of burden." Jesus took all of your burdens upon Himself and set you free from the weight of your sin and burdens. Matthew 11:28-29,

"Come to Me, all *you* who labor and are heavy laden, and I will give you rest.

Take My yoke upon you and learn from Me, for I am gentle and lowly in heart, and you will find rest for your souls." In this scripture, Jesus is referring to two different sets of people. Firstly, He is referring to those who "labor." Those are people who are simply worn out and beat up from life. They are tired from the everyday struggle of existence and have grown weary in all that faces them. Secondly, He addresses those that "are heavy laden."

To be heavy-laden means to have something laid upon you that was not of your choosing, not of your volition, and is not the result of your own decisions or actions. You are suffering under the consequences of somebody else's actions and decisions. That is a burden. That is the definition of burden in this scripture, and the Psalmist has a straightforward solution: "cast your burden on the Lord."

Let it Go: The "casting of your burden" in this scripture is not a casual "surrendering your issues" to the Lord in prayer. This could almost be defined as a "violent release"; it is a passionate letting go of something that you know is dangerous and harmful. We have all seen movies where somebody was handed a live hand grenade or a stick of dynamite that has been lit; that is the picture of this terminology. If you've been given either of these, you are going to get rid of it in a big hurry. You know that if you hang on to it, it will cause significant bodily damage to you. Another illustration would be walking on an enjoyable hike, bending down to pick up a walking stick, and realizing that you just picked up a snake. If you are anything like me, you will not be holding it to admire it, but you will sling it as far away from you as you can, as fast as you can.

Bring your Burdens to the Lord: In this scripture, the Psalmist encourages us to take that same fervent action with those things that burden us. Cast them upon the Lord, throw them off, and refuse to carry them. Many years ago, when I was a youth pastor, I would quite often take a group of youth on short-term mission trips. We had a standing policy that whatever you packed, you carried. We would not allow an individual to pack luggage to the hilt and then expect somebody else to carry it.

It is the same in life. I often tell people that I refuse to carry somebody else's baggage. People often want to dump their issues on others and expect them to carry the weight of those issues. Listen to the Psalmist, bring your burdens to the Lord, and refuse to carry them; you are not designed to. You are, however, intended to live in the sustaining power, ability, and covering of the Lord, and that is His promise over you if you will bring your issues to Him.

The strong, sustaining hand of the Lord is His promise to cover, support, nourish and supply you. It is a no-brainer. Suffer under the weight of somebody else's baggage and endure the harsh consequences of that decision or bring your burden to the Lord and allow Him to cover you, nourish you and cover you with His grace, mercy, forgiveness, and love.

Today's Confession of Peace

In the seasons of the enemy's attacks against me, I choose to rise and stand in faith against his strategies, lies, and weapons.

I put my heart on guard and bring all that concerns me under the loving Lordship of Jesus, to protect my joy and peace. I thank you, Lord, that I have the ability and the discernment to recognize the weapons of warfare that are designed to discourage me, steal my joy and rob my peace.

God has not designed me to carry the weight of my burdens in life. They belong to God, and I choose to cast all of them upon Him. When I am weary and worn out from the issues of life, or when I am under assault from others' actions, I come to the Lord.

I bow my heart and my knee to Him, I declare Him as the Lord of my life and all that concerns me, and I release the stress and the strain of the issues that I am facing. I trust you, Lord. I have every confidence in Your love for me and Your care for me. I thank you that you have a plan and a purpose in all that concerns me and that you will bring your vision to completion as I surrender to you.

Day Twenty-Three

THE UNSEEN PEACE

"So we do not lose heart. Though our outer self is wasting away, our inner self is being renewed day by day. For this light momentary affliction is preparing for us an eternal weight of glory beyond all comparison, as we look not to the things that are seen but to the things that are unseen. For the things that are seen are transient, but the things that are unseen are eternal."

2 Corinthians 4:16-18

You cannot see the subtle difference in your appearance from day to day. In fact, on an on-going basis, nothing seems different each time you look in the mirror. It is not until you see a picture of yourself that may be several months old, a year old or longer, that you see yourself differently. When you see a picture of yourself from the past, it is easy to compare yourself to your present reality and realize that you just might be getting older. Getting older is a reality that all of us must face. I have often said that I do not mind getting "older"; it is getting "old" that I refuse to do. I know people who are years younger than I am, but yet they live old. They see life through old eyes and carry an old perspective. Go ahead, look in the mirror, embrace the reality that you are getting older, but do not lose heart. Do not allow the fact that you are getting older cause you to lose your youthful nature and become an old, grumpy person. Losing heart is to allow your very nature to shift, to change your mode of thinking, and to become troublesome and irritating to those around you.

The Spirit Man: While our outer man is slowly losing vigor and strength, the good news is that our inner man is "being renewed day by day." That is only possible because man is a "triune being," meaning that we are spirit, soul, and body. We are a spirit. We have a soul, and we live in a body. In this scripture, the Apostle Paul refers to the physical, outward body "wasting away." He makes that statement but then says that our inner man is being renewed. Your inner man and the outer man are moving in opposite directions: one is growing weaker while the other is growing stronger. You will eventually come to the place where your inner man is much stronger than your outer man and cannot be contained. That is the day you will depart your terrestrial body and enter into your celestial body.

There is a peace that we can live in even though our outer man is changing. It is a peace that cannot be stolen and is being supernaturally renewed day by day. It is easy to set our eyes on those things before us and allow what we see, think, hear or feel to dictate how we live and determine what is important to us. All around us, we see what the Apostle refers to as "light afflictions," the things that agitate and stress us out. He then brings it all back into reality when he says that those things can work for us and not against us. If we allow the natural life issues to work on our behalf, they can produce an exceeding and eternal weight of glory. Simply put, that means that God will redeem the problems we face in the natural if we allow the renewing peace of our inner man to be the order of the day.

Let Your Soul Breathe: Years ago, I had a friend with a particular affinity for an area of the city we lived in. This area offered shopping venues, cool hangouts, hip eating establishments, theaters, and the like. It was a place that appealed to his generation. He would always make the statement that when he went there, his "soul breathed." While I certainly didn't share his view on that particular part of town, I never lost the phrase that "my soul could breathe."

Based on that, I began to look around my life to find out where my soul could breathe. I discovered that sometimes, it was, in fact, a "place," and other times, it was the moments that I allow my soul to simply catch up with me. Sometimes, it is sitting down to read devotionals, or a book with a good cup of coffee, or sometimes just watch a movie. The point is that I step away from the demands of everyday life and make an investment of rest, peace, and "downtime" into myself. Those are valuable times, and the payoff is enormous.

The Spiritual Diet of the Word: Investing a steady diet of God's word into your spirit and soul also brings much-needed renewal. Only the Word of God can produce the inner renewal that the Psalmist is talking about. Romans 12:2, "And do not be conformed to this world, but be transformed by the renewing of your mind, that you may prove what *is* that good and acceptable and perfect will of God." Mind renewal includes the precious peace of God that will see you through the tumultuous times of life. As you invest a continual diet of His promises into your thought processes and your spiritual man, that word will rise when most needed. In the middle of a conflict or a sudden attack, God's word will be an anchor that will keep your ship from getting hammered by the waves or crashing into the treacherous rocks of life. His Word is His peace.

Today's Confession of Peace

Today, I declare that even though I am getting older, I AM NOT getting old. I will not embrace a mentality of life that keeps me from thinking youthful and fresh.

The Word promises that my youth will be renewed like the eagle. The wrinkles on my face do not betray me; they do not define me but reveal that I am living life to the fullest and that my body struggles to keep up with my spirit.

I am alive, I am active, and I am everything that God's Word says that I am. I have hope and a future, and I will live my days in supernatural peace. My mind is being renewed day by day because of the strength, life, and vitality of the Word of God.

God's Word is strong inside of me, and the supernatural fruit of the Word is that I walk in life, health, abundance, understanding, revelation, and supernatural peace.

I am not moved by what I see around me. I am not disturbed because my outer body grows older day by day. I rejoice in all of the days that God has given me and for those that are yet to come, and I declare today that I will live my life to the fullest until the very last breath that I breathe, and even that breath will be one of great peace and joy, in Jesus' Name.

Day Twenty-Four

THE BEAUTY OF PEACE

"He has made everything beautiful in its time. He has also set eternity in the hearts of men, yet they cannot fathom what God has done from beginning to end."

Ecclesiastes 3:11

You have been shaped, fashioned, and designed by the hand of your Father who deeply loves you, created you with divine purpose, invested His heart into you, and watches over you every single day of your life. As His child, He has promised never to leave you nor forsake you, and the Bible tells us that He delights over you with great joy and even sings over you. I meet so many people in life who feel as if they were just simply born and exist in life only to die. Listen to me. You are not just a biological factor due to a physical relationship between a man and woman. God knew exactly what was going on; He knew that you were needed for such a time as this, and so you were born.

Lessons of Peace

Fearfully and Wonderfully Made: Psalm 139:13-18, "For You formed my inward parts; You covered me in my mother's womb. I will praise You, for I am fearfully *and* wonderfully made; marvelous are Your works, and *that* my soul knows very well. My frame was not hidden from You when I was made in secret and skillfully wrought in the lowest parts of the earth. Your eyes saw my substance, being yet unformed, and in Your book, they all were written, the days fashioned for me when as yet there were none of them. How precious also are Your thoughts to me, O God. How great is the sum of them. If I counted them, they would be more in number than the sand; when I awake, I am still with You."

What does that have to do with peace? Everything. If I feel that somebody is upset with me, particularly a family member, and even more particularly; my wife, I am not at peace. I am disturbed in my emotions, in my spirit, and life does not go on as usual until I have the chance to talk it through and make it right.

He's a Good Father: It is a great feeling knowing that God loves me personally. It feels good knowing that He was intricately involved in shaping and fashioning me, even when I was in my mother's womb. To know that He has fashioned my days and that He only has precious thoughts towards me gives me great peace. To know that He is for me and not against me (Romans 8:31) gives me confidence in life that nothing else can. I have heard it said that God's gift to me was my life and that my gift to Him is what I do with my life. I do not have to wonder if God is mad at me or if He even knows who I am. He does know me, He's not mad at me, and He's excited that I am alive. As the song says, He's a "good, good Father."

Today's Scripture declares that God has "made everything beautiful in it is time." I love the word that is used here in the original Hebrew for "made." It is the word "Asah," and it means that He fashioned and accomplished something. In other words, God sees you as one of His significant accomplishments. When you consider the works of the Lord, the sun, the moon, the earth, the universe, the complicated and intricate designs of His hand, to know that He sees you as one of His outstanding accomplishments is astounding.

That fills my heart with joy, with satisfaction, comfort, and peace. God always takes care of His accomplishments, and you are a masterpiece. He treasures you and values you beyond compare. The love He has for you is beyond any human love that you have ever known. It reaches the highest heaven and the lowest depths.

Lay down in peace tonight, knowing that He is covering you with His great love and that He has already orchestrated your tomorrows. He has already fended off the enemy and ordained your future and your eternity. God wants to spend His eternity with me, which is almost overwhelming but gives me a great peace that nothing else can.

Today's Confession of Peace

I do not just exist. I have been created with great care, great love, and great passion. Even in my mother's womb, God had a plan for my life. I was born because I am part of His great purpose for the earth and all of eternity.

I live in great peace, knowing that God loves me and that I am continually on His mind. He watches over me with great care and has even gone before me and orchestrated my days as well as my eternity.

His passion for me is ceaseless, and even when I feel unloved, unwanted, and unaccepted, I have confidence in knowing that He loves me, wants me, and accepts me. I am one of God's significant accomplishments, and I choose to live my life today as a gift to Him.

I will not walk in fear, I will not walk in rejection, but in the perfect peace of God, in the love of God, and in the fact that I am His and He is mine.

Day Twenty-Five

THE LORD OF PEACE

"May the Lord of peace Himself give you peace at all times and in every way. The Lord be with all of you."

2 Thessalonians 3:16

We serve the God of Shalom. The biblical meaning of peace is: "supernatural tranquility, to be exempt from the rage and havoc of war, peace, harmony, concord, security, safety, prosperity, the blessed state of life." Remember, God does not "possess" those things; He "is" those things. The word "Lord" means that He is the supreme authority and the Sovereign of all. The result of His Lordship over your life is always His peace. It is who He is, and it emanates from His very being and is accessed by your relationship with Him. Have you ever noticed that you tend to talk and behave like the people you are with the most? We all tend to take on characteristics and attributes of those important to us and that we admire. The more time you spend with the Lord, and in His Word, the more you will become like him.

Lessons of Peace

The God Who Gives: When you read the scriptures, no word should be overlooked. In this scripture, even the word "give" is significant. God so loved the world that He "gave." The giving of His Son is the very basis upon which everything else is made available to us. All that you have with God and from Him flows from your relationship with Him. The degree of peace you have from God is determined by the degree of relationship you have with Him. The word "give" means "cause to come forth." Out of your relationship with the Lord, His peace and love come forth. All the things that pertain to life, health, and success come from your relationship with the Lord.

When you read the Word, you can always know that His Word is His will for your life and should be read that way. With that in mind, we can know that God's will for your life is to have peace and to have it in everything that concerns you, at all times and in every way. Remember, Jesus paid a very high price for your peace. Your peace was so important to Him that He died for you to have it. In the Old Testament, God was identified as Jehovah-Shalom, "The Lord is Peace." In the darkest hours of Israel's history, we find that He was a very present peace in the time of need.

In most of the encounters the saints of old had with God, they were instructed to have no fear and to be in peace. Why is that? It is difficult to discern the will of God when you are in fear and have a lack of peace. It is almost impossible to acknowledge and enforce His Lordship in your life when you are battling a lack of peace.

First Things First: God is saying, "first things first." Make me the Lord of your life, enjoy the fullness of your relationship with me, walk in my love and my peace. Just as peace flows out of your relationship with Him, it will also flow into your relationship with others. It can influence circumstantial and situational factors as well. The natural outflow of who you are will permeate and influence whatever you put your hand to. As you go through life, you are going to face complex and challenging situations.

Trusting God, walking in faith with Him, keeping your eyes on Jesus instead of circumstances postures you to see that He can redeem the challenges of life. He will exercise His Lordship over the storms of your life, causing them to work together for good concerning you. God is never caught off guard, and above all things, He wants to be the Lord of Peace over your life and to show Himself strong and faithful on your behalf.

The good news is that He has already purchased your peace. It belongs to you, and nothing that the enemy does can steal it away from you. His peace is your promise, safety, and exemption from the rage and havoc of warfare. God is calling you to the blessed state of life. The blessed life is supernatural peace and abundant life, which results from living under His Lordship.

Today's Confession of Peace

My God is the God of peace. He is never moved by the storms that rage in life or howling winds of adversity or despair. He is above only and never beneath.

Peace flows out of my relationship with my Father, and because of it, I walk in divine harmony, security, tranquility, and supernatural prosperity. I am exempt from the rage and havoc of war. I confess today that God's perfect will for my life and my family is supernatural peace.

No matter what storms may gather, which falsehoods may surface, or strategies that may come into play, I stand steadfast in my relationship with my Father.

The overflow of His heart is shaping me into a person of perfect peace. Out of who I am becoming, I release peace into others around me. People draw peace and harmony from my life.

Circumstances that align themselves against my life must align with peace because I will not stoop to the lies of the enemy or anything that disturbs my peace in Jesus' Name.

Day Twenty-Six

THE SON OF PEACE

"Unto us, a Son is given; And the government will be upon His shoulder. And His name will be called Wonderful, Counselor, Mighty God, Everlasting Father, Prince of Peace."

Isaiah 9:6

I often like to think about what life must have been like on the planet earth before the fall of Adam and Eve. Can you imagine a planet where there was no strife, no sin, and no turmoil? Think about a paradise that was in complete harmony with the purposes of God and where the animals and all of creation were in one accord. Before the fall, this planet was host to regular visits with Father God. Humanity had no concept of confusion, worry, war, poverty, disease, or any of the things that plague our planet today. What I just described is heaven. That is what will be waiting on us when we cross the threshold between earthly life and eternal life. This planet was one of perfect peace. There was no death or decay, but only life and the fullness thereof.

Lessons of Peace

Man's Reign on the Earth: Obviously, that blissful life came to a crashing halt when our very first forefathers decided to take matters into their own hands, and the enemy attempted a failed coup against

God. Man's reign (under God) over the earth ended, and the original plan of creation was marred. But the good news is that God was not finished yet. He had a plan. He crafted a heavenly strategy that would take the earthly kingdom back and establish His reign over the earth once and for all. You know the story, He would send His only Son, Jesus, as a sacrificial lamb, who would pay the eternal ransom that man might be redeemed. Through Jesus, He would restore humanity's authority and reestablish His plans and purposes through His kingdom government. By His obedient life and sacrificial death on the cross, he conquered death, hell, and the grave and brought life to the earth, and opened the door for the kingdom of God to be established in power and authority.

The Rule and Reign of Heaven: What did He restore exactly? In reading the scripture, we find that the prophetic declaration of who Jesus was, also provided a clear description of what He accomplished on the earth and how that affects you and me as believers. When Jesus entered the earthly realm, He brought a new rule and reign with Him. It was the rule and authority of heaven. He would break down the walls erected and bring an end to the law of sin and death and the fear that came with it. The keys were snatched out of the hand of the enemy, and the law of life that is in Christ Jesus would set us free from the dominion and the rule of darkness that had permeated the earth for so long.

Jesus came to set up a new government, one that would be supervised by the Father and would restore the earth to it is rightful leadership. What the first Adam lost; the last Adam regained. But Jesus didn't just come as a ruler over the affairs of the earth; He came to restore the life of the kingdom. He came with a plan revealed in His name; He shall be called: Wonderful, Counselor, Mighty God, Everlasting Father, Prince of Peace. He is a wonderful God. Those are not just accolades but describe who He is. He is marvelous, surpassing all others, extraordinary, separated from all others by His specific actions and life.

There is none like Him, and there never will be. He restored sanctity to the earth, value to life, and dominion back to humanity. As we go down the list of descriptive titles of Jesus, we understand that He is God as a part of the trinity. He cannot be separated from God or the Holy Spirit, and He represents the eternal Godhead, three in one. He is God, but He is also the Son of God. He is the King Eternal, but He is also the Prince of Peace.

Peace Broke the Power of Death: "Prince of Peace" is not just a title; it's a description of who God is. The Father is described as "Jehovah-Shalom," and Jesus is described as "Sarar-Shalom," the Prince of Peace. Sarar is the Hebrew word for Prince, and it means the Lord of peace, the One who holds the power of peace, the one from whom the reign of peace flows. In earthly kingdoms today, rulers strike fear in the hearts of men. Dictators forcibly demand that they be obeyed and followed without question. The penalty for rebellion is automatic punishment and typically death. As the Prince of Peace, Jesus broke the power of death, the lies of fear, and exposed the enemy's weakness as nothing more than a great deception.

We live in this world, but according to the Word of God, we are not of this world. We have no choice but to live here until we make our journey to heaven. Until then, we will live as citizens of the Kingdom of Heaven and not the kingdom of darkness. We have been called out of darkness, out of fear, out of a satanic stronghold, and have been delivered into the light and life of Jesus. We now live by a new set of laws, a new standard of life, with new and exciting directives and mandates for how we should live. We are set free from the law of sin and death and live according to the law of life and peace in Christ Jesus, the Prince of Peace.

Today's Confession of Peace

Thank you, Jesus, for conquering death, hell, and the grave. Thank you for your sacrificial commitment that I might have life and have it in abundance.

You have restored dignity to humanity, and because of the redemptive price you paid for my life, I can live in freedom and walk in the fullness of relationship with my Father, God.

Today, I declare that You are marvelous; your majesty surpasses all others. You are extraordinary and are separated from all others by Your life. There is none like You, and there never will be.

You have restored sanctity to the earth, value to life, and dominion back to humanity. I have been called out of darkness, out of fear, out of a satanic stronghold, and have been delivered into the light and life of Jesus.

I am set free from the law of sin and death and now live according to the law of life and peace in Christ Jesus, the Prince of Peace.

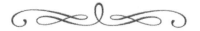

Day Twenty-Seven

THE MOUNTAIN OF PEACE

"For the mountains shall depart And the hills be removed,
But My kindness shall not depart from you, Nor shall My covenant of
peace be removed," Says the Lord, who has mercy on you."
Isaiah 54:10

Our Father is Jehovah-Shalom, the God of all peace. It is important to remember that God's names are not just what we call Him but describe who He is. Remember, God does not *possess* peace, He *is* peace. He is the ultimate source of peace and the originator of peace. It is His character, the very essence of His being. God's desire for you is peace, even in an ever-changing world that is continually the source of hurt, betrayal, and disappointment. All of us have placed our trust in someone or something only to be let down. We have all had to deal with the remnants of broken relationships or even good intentions that have gone bad. Unfortunately, broken hearts are something that most of us are familiar with. The good news is that God has a plan for your restoration and recovery.

Lessons of Peace

The Word of Covenant: I love the mountains. If my family is discussing a vacation, my vote is always for the mountains. I find a certain strength in the mountains and a serenity that I find nowhere else. The majesty of the mountains speaks volumes of the greatness of creation. It is where "my soul can breathe." But even the mountains have no guarantee of longevity. I have seen beautiful mountainous regions cut down to make way for "progress."

I have seen landslides where mountainsides collapse and reshape. I have seen the result of years of wind and rain and can only imagine what the mountain used to look like. We can see that even the mountains are susceptible to the shifting sands of time or the decisions of individuals who have a "better idea." The Bible says that "heaven and earth will pass away, but my words will never pass away" (Matthew 24:35). What are His words? His words are His covenant. His covenant is His heart that is revealed in His passion and His commitment to you. It is a never-ending covenant that cannot and will not be broken.

The Promise of Redemption: God's covenant promise over you is the promise of redemption. His covenant over you is steadfast and irrevocable. Your covenant is a source of moral and spiritual power and your access to the Father and all of His benefits. By covenant, God has bound Himself to sustain you, sanctify you and cover you with grace, favor, and blessing in return for our commitment to serving Him with all of our hearts. As you walk in obedience to the Word, you enjoy a never-ending flow of covenantal blessings as promised to us in the Word.

It is through His covenant with us that He can bestow His divine influence upon us and flow into every arena of our lives by His Spirit.

The Promise of Peace: One of the greatest covenant promises that we have is that of peace. He promises that His kindness will never depart from us, and the covenant of peace will never be removed. The kindness of God is the faithfulness of God. Think about that. I have a promise from God that He will always be faithful to me. He will never leave me nor forsake me. The kindness of God towards me means that He will lift me above reproach out of His faithfulness and not allow me to live in shame.

He has redeemed me from the snare of the fowler, from the power of sin, and the effects of sin in my life. My past has been redeemed, and I am no longer held responsible for sins that have been forgiven. I never have to answer that which is under the blood. When the storms of my past arise, the Lord declares over that storm: "Peace, be still."

The Precious Blood: Biblical covenants are based on the blood. By the blood of Jesus, the curse of sin and death has been broken off me, and I am reconciled to the Father. Through that reconciliation, the Covenant of Peace was instituted once and for all. The Covenant of Peace is the very basis for the Gospel of Peace, and that Gospel (the good news) is the foundation for a heart that is overflowing with peace. The Covenant of Peace means that I can live in an intimate relationship with God, who loves me unconditionally. It means that I can trust Him with every aspect of my life: past, present, and future; spirit, soul, and body.

Peace becomes the standard by which everything else is measured. I do not have to bring the standard of the covenant into my life; I bring my life into the standard of the covenant of peace. In other words, the parameters by which I live my life are determined by the covenant of peace. If there is no peace, it is not covenant, if it does not create peace, it is not covenant, and if it is not covenant, it is not God.

Today's Confession of Peace

Even when I see the mountains tremble and the nations shake, I will not fear, and I will not be moved. Though all around me I see the "hills be removed," I will not be shaken. My God is an everlasting God and the God of an eternal covenant.

His promises over me are yes, and amen and cannot be destroyed. Though the heathen rage and though the earth is shaken, my God is a faithful, trustworthy, and just God, and His mercies are new every morning.

He is the God who sustains me, sanctifies me, and covers me with grace, favor, and blessing. I choose today to stand before the Lord in obedience to His Word and bask in the favor of His covenantal benefits as they flow in my life as promised by the Word.

I walk in the strength of the Covenant of Peace, and by the blood of Jesus, the curse of sin is broken, and I am reconciled to my Father for all eternity.

Today, I enjoy peace, I walk in peace, and my life is founded upon peace. Peace is the standard by which I live.

Day Twenty-Eight

COME UNTO ME

"Come to Me, all you who labor and are heavy laden, and I will give you rest. Take My yoke upon you and learn from Me, for I am gentle and lowly in heart, and you will find rest for your souls. For My yoke is easy, and My burden is light."

Matthew 11:28-30

Many factors set Christianity apart from other world religions. The greatest is that Jesus intentionally came to serve humanity and to demonstrate the love of the Father in such a dynamic way that He sacrificed His own life. Matthew 20:28, "I did not come to be served, but to serve, and give my life as a ransom to many." As you already know, Jesus gave of Himself; spirit, soul, and body so that you might enjoy eternal life with the Father. It is also important to remember that He is intimately concerned about your complete well-being and made full, relational provision for how you live your life daily. Christianity is not only about securing an eternal home in heaven but also living the abundant life that God has destined for you, right here on earth.

In the World, But not of the World: The tension that most Christians feel is that even though we are not "of this world," we are still "in this world." We are affected regularly by the issues of life, the warfare of the kingdom, and the actions of those around us. Even though we walk in the rights and privileges of the kingdom of God, we are still susceptible to the natural elements of our world. We must come to the place where we acknowledge the trials and tribulations created by the tactics of the enemy and learn to walk in the covering promised us by our covenant.

In this verse, Jesus makes an amazing appeal to those who are weary and worn out from life issues. In His kind and loving invitation, He reveals the compassionate heart of a Savior who is deeply committed to your health and well-being. Coming to Jesus means that there must be a letting go of the things that produces grief and turmoil in your life. To benefit from the kindness and care of the Lord, you must let go of the brokenness and hurt that continues to drive you away from His loving kindness and tender mercies.

Come, Now: His call is to hurting humanity and specifically to those who "labor." The Greek word is "Kuopio," and it carries the meaning of those that are weary, tired, exhausted, and burdened with the toils of life. We have all been there. Life can be challenging, and it can be exhausting. The unexpected circumstances of life can knock the wind out of your sails and leave you holding nothing but prayer. When you find yourself in that place, the call is to come. It is an imperative command and is issued with an urgent appeal. Come, now. I have a place where you can find restoration, recover from your weariness, collect your strength and discover refreshing, but you have to let go.

The second group to whom Jesus calls out are those that are heavy "laden." That word is "Phortizo" and conveys the sense of being under a heavy weight and burden that somebody else has placed upon you. It is not a weight that results from your own decisions or actions, but those of others. The heavy weight of Phortizo is the sudden death of a precious one, a phone call in the middle of the night, a lost job, a divorce, an unexpected bill, and the list goes on. Much like the toils of life, we have all been there as well. We have all suffered under the heavy hand of somebody else's decisions, actions, and lack of consideration. Jesus has a word for you: come. "Come and let Me breathe life into your weary soul," says the Lord. "Come and allow Me to put My yoke upon you."

Take My Yoke: The "yoke" of the Lord is the life of His word. It is in His word that you find life and health, peace and blessing and rest. Allowing the Word to wash over you and bring refreshing to your mind, your soul, and even your body is the heart cry of the Lord. The yoking of the Lord is how He comes alongside you and carries the weight of your burden on your behalf. It is also the process of teaching you how to walk and live when life's pressures come against you. When a farmer yokes up two oxen, he will always join an older, wiser, and seasoned veteran with a young "buck" who hasn't learned the ropes yet. The process of yoking is what Jesus means when He says, "take My yoke upon you and learn of Me."

Jesus is inviting you into a relationship with Himself. He is reaching out to you with a passion and a love that transcends the pressures of life that you are facing. He cares about you and your circumstances, and He stands ready and waiting to surround you with grace, mercy, and every good thing that you need to rise and be a victor and not a victim.

Today's Confession of Peace

Lord, today I want to thank you that you love me and that you are intimately involved in every area of my life. I am grateful for your mercy and your kindness that I find new every morning.

Thank you for the provision that you made for me that I might not only have eternal life but that I might live in the abundance of your word now.

I know that I am not of this world, but I do live in this world, and while I face pressures on every side, I set myself in complete agreement and accord with your plans and purposes for my life.

I come to you. I run to you in the toils of life when I find myself under the weight of others' actions. When I am weak, you are strong; when I am lost, you are my way.

I choose today to yoke myself to you and your word. I saturate my mind, my heart, and my speech with the life of your Word.

I will learn of you and follow hard after you to become more like you in all that I do and in who I am.

Day Twenty-Nine

A KINGDOM OF PEACE

"For the kingdom of God is not eating and drinking, but righteousness and peace and joy in the Holy Spirit. For he who serves Christ in these things is acceptable to God and approved by men. Therefore let us pursue the things which make for peace and the things by which one may edify another."

Romans 14:17-19

As a believer, you have been called out of darkness and into the marvelous light of His love (1 Peter 2:9). That makes you a citizen of the Kingdom of God. The kingdoms of men come and go, rise and fall, and in their wake either contribute significantly to humanity or are a scourge of fallen man. History is laden with tales of great leaders who inspired their followers and made a difference in those who followed them. It also tells of those who led by fear, destroyed and held captive those who followed them.

Lessons of Peace

The Two Kingdoms: Outside of the kingdoms of man, there are only two kingdoms: the Kingdom of God and the kingdom of darkness. They are spiritual kingdoms and very real but are neither geographical nor political. Every person that exists or has ever existed belongs to one of these kingdoms. Kingdoms exist in the hearts of every person. There is no kingdom without a king who has been crowned and enthroned as a ruler. Every kingdom has a territory or a realm over which the king rules and every kingdom has citizens.

The citizens of any particular kingdom abide by and adhere to the laws and the customs of the kingdom to which they belong. Every kingdom has strengths and powers and also has a particular purpose and destiny. In the Kingdom of God, Jesus is the King; heaven is the realm, and believers are the citizens. The law of the Kingdom of God is the Word of God, and destiny is heaven. The two kingdoms stand in stark contrast to one another.

Kingdom Character: The kingdom of God itself is not tangible in terms of geographical lands and buildings; however, it does manifest in real ways that impact citizens' lives of both kingdoms. In this scripture, the Apostle Paul identifies God's kingdom's three specific attributes: righteousness, peace, and joy in the Holy Spirit. There are significant benefits to being a citizen of God's kingdom, the attributes that flow out of a relationship with the King.

You have access to these benefits, which eventually become a part of your character. The Kingdom character that you possess will influence how you live, how you see life and will affect the four primary gates of your life: what you see, think, hear and feel. When kingdom dynamics are ruling and reigning in your life, you will perceive the gates through a kingdom mentality. For example, religious people will see the lost of the world and become disgusted with them. On the other hand, Jesus saw the lost of the world, perceived them through kingdom character, and identified them as "white unto harvest" (John 4:35). See the difference?

Kingdom Attributes: The Apostle Paul identifies three specific attributes that readily mark citizens of God's kingdom. To be righteous is to have integrity, virtue, and purity of life and a healthy balance of emotions that manifest in how you act and live. God is righteous, and His children become righteous after Him in like manner. It is always a righteous response that dissipates darkness and turns back the tide of evil doing.

The world tells you to "fight fire with fire," but the kingdom of God tells you to "Love your enemies, do good to those who hate you, bless those who curse you, and pray for those who spitefully use you. To him who strikes you on the *one* cheek, offer the other also. And from him who takes away your cloak, do not withhold *your* tunic either. Give to everyone who asks of you. And from him who takes away your goods do not ask *them* back. And just as you want men to do to you, you also do to them likewise" (Luke 6:27-31).

Set your Heart to the Kingdom: Flowing out of the kingdom is a peace and joy that the world cannot replicate. The kingdom of darkness is predicated on lies because the lord of that kingdom is the father of lies. Due to the absence of an authentic peace or joy, the citizens of that kingdom are prone to seek after false substitutes that only serve to ensnare further and bring them into captivity. Abuse and addictions that create years of bondage and servitude are rampant within the kingdom of darkness.

Only God can give true, lasting peace that stands against the wiles of the enemy and produces joy even when all hell is breaking out. This scripture tells us to "pursue the things which make for peace." In other words, set your heart to the kingdom. You will not find what you are looking for and what you need anywhere else. The prodigal son spent all that he had looking for satisfaction and in pursuit of the pleasures of life, but at the end of the day, what he needed was found in the kingdom of his father. The very thing that he had forsaken was the same thing that would be his deliverance (Luke 15:11-32). The kingdom of darkness can only offer brokenness and waste, but God offers you a robe, a ring, and righteousness that produces true and lasting peace and joy.

Today's Confession of Peace

I have been called out of darkness and into the marvelous light of God's love. I am a "called out one." My life has been marked with glory and purpose.

I have been set apart for kingdom design and kingdom purpose. I have a kingdom mentality that shapes how I see, think, feel and hear. I am not typical, I am not ordinary, but I am a supernatural product of God's love in my life.

I have been rescued by God, and I have a pure and passionate relationship with the King. He loves me and is passionate about who I am and who I am becoming.

I walk in kingdom character that manifests itself in purposeful righteousness, joy, and peace that surpasses understanding. Today, I will wholeheartedly pursue those things that make for peace.

I will set my mind to think thoughts that are godly, pure, and holy. I will not waste the valuable years of my life, seeking after that which is nothing more than a false substitute for the riches waiting for me in my relationship with the King.

Day Thirty

PEACE THAT CRUSHES SATAN

"For your obedience has become known to all. Therefore I am glad on your behalf, but I want you to be wise in what is good and simple concerning evil. And the God of peace will crush Satan under your feet shortly. The grace of our Lord Jesus Christ be with you. Amen."

Romans 16:19-20

Over the years, I have often heard well-meaning Christians give pet nicknames to the devil. People often refer to him as "ol' slew foot" and other names that tend to mask the reality that he is the archenemy of your soul and has a diabolical plan to destroy everything you are about. The Word is very clear in John 10:10 that the enemy comes to "steal, kill and destroy," but Jesus has come that you might have life and have it abundantly. As believers, we must be aware that the enemy's power is nothing more than a lie. Indeed, his lies manifest themselves into very real and dangerous scenarios when people begin to act on the lies. But once the lie is broken, the manifestations will cease. Only God is all-knowing and all-powerful. The devil is a created being, and his power is limited and finite. He was utterly defeated at the cross when the power and authority that he usurped from Adam in the garden was taken away from him and rightfully restored to Christ.

Lessons of Peace

Under Your Feet: We have all seen cartoons that portray a demonic entity on one shoulder and an angelic entity on the other, with both giving their suggestive advice. Many people buy into that scenario or believe that they are in the middle of a spiritual tug of war with God pulling on one side and Satan pulling on the other. Neither of those representations are accurate or biblical. The problem with both of those considerations is that it puts God, Satan, and humanity on the same level. In no way will God and Satan ever be on the same level, and neither will you and Satan. God is exalted over all, and above all, and man is exalted over Satan. Most Christians find it hard to believe, but the truth of the Gospel is that you are more powerful than the devil, and He is under your authority.

Supernatural Peace: God is the one who crushes Satan, and He does it under your feet. What does that mean? You and I have a place in God whereby we operate in the power and authority of His Word, and all of the powers of hell cannot stand against it. Satanic lies cannot penetrate or disrupt God's supernatural peace, and when you stay in peace, you trample his schemes, strategies, and systems. The enemy wants to get you out of peace and into fear to separate you from the power of the anointing that destroys every yoke of bondage. Your peace is supernatural, and it is powerful enough to bruise Satan and his minions under your feet.

In the Old Testament, God told Joshua that every place his feet would "tread," He would give to him (Joshua 1:3). That is much more than a simple walk around a great walled city; it is the military term "darak," which means to exercise warfare. So, Joshua is saying wherever you exercise the authority that you have in Me; I will give you the victory. Your peace is a great weapon that the Lord will use against your enemies and on your behalf. Most people never see peace as a weapon, but God says that He will use it to crush Satan underneath your feet. There is an authority in the peace of God and a confidence that allows you to walk as the redeemed and to tread over the works of darkness. Your victory is your peace, and your peace is your victory.

Today's Confession of Peace

I make no room in my life for the activity of the enemy. I am not a victim of his lies and deceit, and I no longer live under the bondage of sin. I am free, and I walk in the freedom of life and the victory that is in the Word.

Today, I choose to stand in the authority of peace and the power of God's promises over me. I am not a victim but a victor in Christ.

I resist the satanic strongholds and lies that arise against me, and I make my mark in the kingdom by faith, and the abundant life of God in Christ Jesus is manifesting in all that I put my hands to.

I have power and authority, and the greater one lives on the inside of me, and His peace is the determining factor to how I live, who I am, and the fulfillment of my destiny and purpose. I celebrate the victory that I have today because the God of peace is crushing Satan underneath my feet.

Day Thirty-One

PEACE DURING CRISIS

"For we do not wrestle against flesh and blood, but against principalities, against powers, against the rulers of the darkness of this age, against spiritual hosts of wickedness in the heavenly places. Therefore take up the whole armor of God that you may be able to withstand in the evil day, and having done all, to stand. Stand therefore, having girded your waist with truth, having put on the breastplate of righteousness, and having shod your feet with the preparation of the gospel of peace; above all, taking the shield of faith with which you will be able to quench all the fiery darts of the wicked one. And take the helmet of salvation, and the sword of the Spirit, which is the word of God."
Ephesians 6:12-17

Remember, peace is not an emotion, rather, it is your position in Christ. Because Christ is in you and you are in Christ, you are also in peace. That is the good news, the gospel. During a crisis, I must remember to put on my good news shoes, which is the gospel of peace. These shoes have a dual purpose - they are both offensive as well as defensive. Suppose you are going to extinguish the flaming darts (accusations) of the enemy. In that case, it will be because you take your place of confidence and exercise readiness whenever the attacks come. Being firmly rooted in a position of unshakeable peace is one of the essential parts of your armor. A soldier's footgear was very much like our modern-day cleats that athletes wear. It was critical to keep balanced. No matter how intact the rest of his armor, he was susceptible to the enemy if he lost his footing. It is the same with us today. If you lose your peace, it is almost guaranteed that the enemy will gain an advantage over you, and the battle will swing in his direction.

The Defense of Peace: Much like the sword of the Spirit (the Word of God), the shoes of peace have a dual-action ability and intention. Our "peace defense" is our conviction and confidence in our position in Christ. No matter how difficult the circumstances may become, we remain in a place of peace, knowing that the grace of God covers us. His purposes go before us, and the blood defeats the enemy. We stand firm on the power of the Word and the promises of the Word that "the battle is not ours, but the Lord's." "Watch, stand fast in the faith, be brave, be strong. Let all that you do be done with love" (1 Corinthians 16:13-14).

Our peace is also an offensive weapon designed to keep you one step ahead of the battle. Boldly declaring the Word in faith, confidence and peace establishes the Word's strength regardless of the lies and strategies of the enemy that have come against you. "I will go before you and make the mountains level. I will break the doors of bronze in pieces and cut apart the bars of iron" (Isaiah 45:2). Standing on the peace of the Word allows you to defend your territory. Releasing the peace of the Word through your strong confession of faith will enable you to charge into the territory of the enemy and take back what rightfully belongs to you. "Fear not, for I am with you; be not dismayed, for I am your God. I will strengthen you, yes, I will help you, I will uphold you with My righteous right hand" (Isaiah 41:10).

God is for You, Not Against You: None of us are exempt from the enemy's attacks. You will never arrive at a place in your life where your faith, righteousness, and redemptive rights go unchallenged. The key is to be continually on guard and in an ever-ready state of mind for when the battles do come, and they will. Remember, God is always for you and never against you. He is on your side and has already gone ahead of you to prepare how He would have you go.

The destination has already been determined, the journey has already been established, and now the walk begins. Walk strong, walk in faith, confidence, and peace. Your destiny is a valuable and precious treasure, and the enemy does not want you to fulfill it. He works hard to keep you from your destiny and is determined to paralyze you with fear and immobilize you with lies that will disrupt your peace.

The Anointing of Peace: You have an anointing of peace on your life. God's plan of peace has been bought and paid for by the precious blood of Jesus. Stress, anxiety, depression, rejection, and turmoil are all tools of the enemy or are emotional reactions that the power of peace must address. Flood your mind and fill your heart with God's declaration of peace over you. Isaiah 59:19, "When the enemy comes in like a flood, The Spirit of the LORD will lift a standard against him." That standard is peace, and it transcends understanding. It is more significant than all of the enemy's power, and it belongs to you because you belong to God.

Today's Confession of Peace

I am firmly rooted and planted in the courts of my God, and I walk in the good news shoes of peace. I am not shaken or moved even when the enemy launches his attacks against me.

I stand in confidence and readiness, and I am not susceptible to the strategies that have been designed to defeat me. Jesus is Lord over who I am, spirit, soul, and body. My emotions are intact, I am a healthy believer, and I wear my armor well.

God goes before me in all that I do. He is my fortress, my tower, and my stronghold. He levels the mountains before me, He breaks down the doors of bronze, and He cuts apart the bars of iron by the power and the authority of His word.

I will not walk in fear, but in faith only. I will not be moved from my place of peace, even when the enemy challenges my redemptive rights. I stand steadfast in the confidence that I have in God's destiny on my life.

The standard of God's love, grace, and peace surround me on every side, and I am what the Word says I am, I have what the Word says I have, and I am determined to accept nothing less than the very best of God for my life, my family and my future.

ABOUT THE AUTHOR

Scott Reece is a man who is passionate about the Word of God. In full-time ministry since 1978, he has served as a USAF Chaplain's Assistant, youth pastor, church planter and as a denominational district supervisor for thirteen years in the Southeastern United States, as a pastor to pastors. Currently serving as the lead pastor of River City Church in Moline, Illinois, Pastor Scott is leading a congregation that is impacting a community, a nation and a world.

As a father of six children, and grandfather of two grandchildren, his passion is to see the next generation rise up and embrace the truth and integrity of the Word of God and change the world through the Word.

Made in the USA
Monee, IL
19 April 2023

32061132R00085